A JOURNEY OF RICHES

Awaken to Your Inner Truth

12 Insights to deepen your inner connection

Published by Motion Media International
Editors: Kit Brookman, Tiffany Oharo, Calvary Diggs, and Kate Tinker
Proofreader: Matthew Dunne
Cover Design: Motion Media International
Typesetting & Assembly: Motion Media International
Printing: Amazon and Ingram Sparks

Creator: John Spender - Primary Author
Title: *A Journey of Riches - Awaken to Your Inner Truth*
ISBN Digital: 978-1-925919-41-7
ISBN Print: 978-1-925919-42-4
Subjects: Motivation, Inspiration, Spirituality

ACKNOWLEDGMENTS

Reading and writing is a gift that very few give to themselves. It is such a powerful way to reflect and gain closure from the past; reading and writing is a therapeutic process. The experience raises one's self-esteem, confidence and awareness of self.

I learned this when I collated the first book in the *A Journey of Riches* series, which now includes twenty-eight books with over 300 co-authors from more than forty different countries. It's difficult to write about your personal experiences, and I honor and respect every author who has collaborated in the series.

For many of the authors, English is their second language, which is a significant achievement. In creating this anthology of short stories, I have been touched by the generosity, gratitude and shared energy this experience has given everyone.

The inspiration for A Journey of Riches, Awaken to Your Inner Truth was born from my own struggles with listening to the voice in my head over the wisdom whispering from my heart. This book serves as a reminder to trust the answers from deep within ourselves.

I want to thank all the authors for entrusting me with their unique memories, encounters and wisdom. Thank you for sharing and opening the door to your soul so others may learn from your experience. I trust the readers will gain confidence from your successes, and wisdom, from your failures.

I also want to thank my family. I know you are proud of me, seeing how far I have come from that ten-year-old boy learning how to read and write at a basic level. Big shout out to my Mom, Robert, Dad, Merril; my brother Adam and his daughter Krystal;

Acknowledgments

my sister Hollie, her partner Brian, my nephew Charlie and niece, Heidi; thank you for your support. Also, kudos to my grandparents, Gran and Pop, who are alive and well, and Ma and Pa, who now rest in peace. They accept me just the way I am with all my travels and adventures around the world.

Thanks to all the team at Motion Media International; you have done an excellent job at editing and collating this book. It was a pleasure working with you on this successful project, and I thank you for your patience in dealing with the various changes and adjustments along the way.

Thank you, the reader, for having the courage to look at your life and how you can improve your future in a fast and rapidly changing world.

Thank you again to my fellow co-authors: Casey Plouffe, Andrew Geldert, Angela Orora Medway-Smith, Anne Henning, Grit Sanders, Helle Lisle, Hugh Dinning, JeNeil Miles, Sandra Elston, Suzie Curiel, and Ivan Budiani.

We would greatly appreciate an honest review on Amazon if this book inspires you. This is how we gain more readers to find our inspiring book!

With gratitude,
John Spender

Praise For *A Journey of Riches* Book Series

"The *A Journey of Riches* book series is a great collection of inspiring short stories that will leave you wanting more!"
~ Alex Hoffmann, Network Marketing Guru.

"If you are looking for an inspiring read to get you through any change, this is it! This book is comprised of many gripping perspectives from a collection of successful international authors with a tone of wisdom to share."
~ TheeraPhetmalaigul, Entrepreneur/Investor.

"*A Journey of Riches* is an empowering series that implements two simple words in overcoming life's struggles.
By diving into the meaning of the words "problem" and "challenge," you will find yourself motivated to believe in the triumph of perseverance. With many different authors from all around the world coming together to share various stories of life's trials, you will find yourself drenched in encouragement to push through even the darkest of battles. The stories are heartfelt personal shares of moving through and transforming challenges into rich life experiences.

The book will move, touch and inspire your spirit to face and overcome any of life's adversities. It is a truly inspirational read. Thank you for being the kind, open soul you are, John!"
~ Casey Plouffe, Seven Figure Network Marketer.

"A must-read for anyone facing major changes or challenges in life right now. This book will give you the courage to move through any struggle with confidence, grace and ease."
~ Jo-Anne Irwin, Transformational Coach and Best Selling Author.

"I have enjoyed the *Journey of Riches* book series. Each person's story is written from the heart, and everyone's journey is different. We all have a story to tell, and John Spender does an amazing job of finding authors and combining their stories into uplifting books."
~ Liz Misner Palmer, Foreign Service Officer.

"A timely read as I'm facing a few challenges right now. I like the various insights from the different authors. This book will inspire you to move through any challenge or change that you are experiencing."
~ David Ostrand, Business Owner.

"I've known John Spender for a while now, and I was blessed with an opportunity to be in book four in the series. I know that you will enjoy this new journey, like the rest of the books in the series. The collection of stories will assist you with making changes, dealing with challenges and seeing that transformation is possible for your life."
~ Charlie O' Shea, Entrepreneur.

"*A Journey of Riches* series will draw you in and help you dig deep into your soul. These authors have unbelievable life stories of purpose inside of them. John Spender is dedicated to bringing peace, love and adventure to the world of his readers! Dive into this series, and you will be transformed!"
~ JeanaMatichak, Author of *Finding Peace*.

"Awesome! Truly inspirational! It is amazing what the human spirit can achieve and overcome! Highly recommended!"
~ FabriceBeliard, Australian Business Coach and Best Selling Author.

"*A Journey of Riches* Series is a must-read. It is an empowering collection of inspirational and moving stories, full of courage, strength and heart. Bringing peace and awareness to those lucky enough to read to assist and inspire them on their life journey."
~ Gemma Castiglia, Avalon Healing, Best Selling Author.

"The *A Journey of Riches* book series is an inspirational collection of books that will empower you to take on any challenge or change in life."
~ Kay Newton, Midlife Stress Buster, and Best Selling Author.

"*A Journey of Riches* book series is an inspiring collection of stories, sharing many different ideas and perspectives on how to overcome challenges, deal with change and make empowering choices in your life. Open the book anywhere and let your mood choose where you need to read. Buy one of the books today; you'll be glad that you did!"
~ Trish Rock, Modern Day Intuitive, Best Selling Author, Speaker, Psychic & Holistic Coach.

"*A Journey of Riches*is another inspiring read. The authors are from all over the world, and each has a unique perspective to share that will have you thinking differently about your current circumstances in life. An insightful read!"
~ Alexandria Calamel, Success Coach and Best Selling Author.

"The *A Journey of Riches* book series is a collection of real-life stories, which are truly inspiring and give you the confidence that no matter what you are dealing with in your life, there is a light at the end of the tunnel, and a very bright one at that. Totally empowering!"
~ John Abbott, Freedom Entrepreneur.

"An amazing collection of true stories from individuals who have overcome great changes, and who have transformed their lives and used their experience to uplift, inspire and support others."
~ Carol Williams, Author, Speaker & Coach.

"You can empower yourself from the power within this book that can help awaken the sleeping giant within you. John has a purpose in life to bring inspiring people together to share their wisdom for the benefit of all who venture deep into this book series. If you are looking for inspiration to be someone special, this book can be your guide."
~ Bill Bilwani, Renowned Melbourne Restaurateur.

"In the *A Journey of Riches* series, you will catch the impulse to step up, reconsider and settle for only the very best for yourself and those around you. Penned from the heart and with an unflinching drive to make a difference for the good of all, *A Journey of Riches* series is a must-read."
~ Steve Coleman, author of *Decisions, Decisions! How to Make the Right One Every Time.*

"Do you want to be on top of your game? *A Journey of Riches* is a must-read with breakthrough insights that will help you do just that!"
~ Christopher Chen, Entrepreneur.

"In *A Journey of Riches*, you will find the insight, resources and tools you need to transform your life. By reading the author's stories, you, too, can be inspired to achieve your greatest accomplishments and what is truly possible for you. Reading this book activates your true potential for transforming your life way beyond what you think is possible. Read it and learn how you, too, can have a magical life."
~ Elaine Mc Guinness, Best Selling Author of *Unleash Your Authentic Self!*

"If you are looking for an inspiring read, look no further than the *A Journey of Riches* book series. The books are an inspiring collection of short stories that will encourage you to embrace life even more. I highly recommend you read one of the books today!"
~ Kara Dono, Doula, Healer and Best Selling Author.

"*A Journey of Riches* series is a must-read for anyone seeking to enrich their own lives and gain wisdom through the wonderful stories of personal empowerment & triumphs over life's challenges. I've given several copies to my family, friends and clients to inspire and support them to step into their greatness. I highly recommend that you read these books, savoring the many 'aha's' and tools you will discover inside."
~ Michele Cempaka, Hypnotherapist, Shaman, Transformational Coach & Reiki Master.

"If you are looking for an inspirational read, look no further than the *A Journey of Riches* book series. The books are an inspiring and educational collection of short stories from the author's soul that will encourage you to embrace life even more. I've even given them to my clients, too, so that their journeys inspire them in life for wealth, health and everything else in between. I recommend you make it a priority to read one of the books today!"
~ Goro Gupta, Chief Education Officer, Mortgage Terminator, Property Mentor.

"The *A Journey of Riches* book series is filled with real-life short stories of heartfelt tribulations turned into uplifting, self-transformation by the power of the human spirit to overcome adversity. The journeys captured in these books will encourage you to embrace life in a whole new way. I highly recommend reading this inspiring anthology series."
~ Chris Drabenstott, Best Selling Author, and Editor.

"There is so much motivational power in the *A Journey of Riches* series!! Each book is a compilation of inspiring, real-life stories by several different authors, which makes the journey feel more relatable and success more attainable. If you are looking for something to move you forward, you'll find it in one (or all) of these books."
~ Cary MacArthur, Personal Empowerment Coach.

"I've been fortunate to write with John Spender, and now, I call him a friend. *A Journey of Riches* book series features real stories that have inspired me and will inspire you. John has a passion for finding amazing people from all over the world, giving the series a global perspective on relevant subject matters."
~ Mike Campbell, Fat Guy Diary, LLC.

"The *A Journey of Riches* series is the reflection of beautiful souls who have discovered the fire within. Each story takes you inside the truth of what truly matters in life. While reading these stories, my heart space expanded to understand that our most significant contribution in this lifetime is to give and receive love. May you also feel inspired as you read this book."

~ Katie Neubaum, Author of *Transformation Calling*.

"*A Journey of Riches* is an inspiring testament that love and gratitude are the secret ingredients to living a happy and fulfilling life. This series is sure to inspire and bless your life in a big way. Truly an inspirational read that is written and created by real people, sharing real-life stories about the power and courage of the human spirit."

~ Jen Valadez, Emotional Intuitive and Best Selling Author.

TABLE OF CONTENTS

Chapter Ten

Awakening to My Inner Purpose

Chapter Eleven

Being Human

Chapter Twelve

Free at Last

PREFACE

I collated this book and chose authors from around the world to share their experiences about what "awaken to inner truth" meant to them. The eclectic collection of chapters encompass a myriad of different writing styles and perspectives that embrace the intelligence of our hearts and intuition.

Like all of us, each author has a unique story and insight to share with you. It might so happen that one or more authors have lived through an experience like circumstances in your life. Their words could be just the words you need to read to help you through your challenges and motivate you to continue your chosen path.

Storytelling has been the way humankind has communicated ideas and learning throughout our civilization. While we have become more sophisticated with technology and living in the modern world is more convenient, there is still much discontent and dissatisfaction. Many people have also moved away from reading books, and they are missing valuable information that can help them move forward in life with a positive outlook. Moving towards the tasks or dreams that scare us breeds confidence growing towards becoming better versions of ourselves.

I think it is essential to turn off the television, slow down, read, reflect, and take the time to appreciate everything you have in life. Start with an anthology book as they offer a cornucopia of viewpoints relating to a particular theme. Here, it's fear and how others have dealt with it. I think we feel stuck in life or having challenges in a particular area because we see the problem through the same lens that created it. With this compendium and all the books in the *A Journey of Riches* series, you have many writing styles and perspectives that will help you think and see your challenges differently, motivating you to elevate your set of circumstances.

Anthology books are also great because you can start from any chapter and gain valuable insight or a nugget of wisdom without the feeling you have missed something from the earlier episodes.

I love reading many different types of personal development books because learning and personal growth are vital. If you are not learning and growing, well, you're staying the same. Everything in the universe is growing, expanding, and changing. If we are not open to different ideas and a multitude of ways to think and be, then even the most skilled and educated among us can become close-minded.

The concept of this book series is to open you up to diverse ways of perceiving your reality. It is to encourage you and give you many avenues of thinking about the same subject. My wish for you is to feel empowered to make a decision that will best suit you in moving forward with your life. As Albert Einstein said, **"We cannot solve problems with the same level of thinking that created them."** With Einstein's words in mind, let your mood pick a chapter in the book, or read from the beginning to the end and be guided to find the answers you seek.

If you feel inspired, we would love an honest review on Amazon. This will help create awareness around this fantastic series of books.

With gratitude,
John Spender

"Awaken to your potential and live the life of your dreams."

~ Unknown

CHAPTER ONE

Inner Communion

By Casey Plouffe

This chapter is dedicated to the lightworkers of Earth. Thank you for being willing to be seen in your authentic inner light and truth. Your authenticity is a medicine that strengthens my courage, and for that, I am eternally grateful. I'll meet you in the garden.

> "This above all: to thine own self be true."
> — William Shakespeare, Hamlet

Have you ever been fucked in the jungle? Allow me to describe my experience.

After listening to my soul's call for help, I ended up in the jungle of Central America, where I was gifted with teachings from various indigenous cultures. I journeyed to the wilderness to work with the medicine of my own breath, and it led me to the many medicines of Earth's mothering vibration of natural elements. In 2016, I wrote about my first experience of elevating to a higher vibrational frequency as a co-author of the international bestselling book A Journey of Riches: Making Changes, when I set the intention to journey even deeper into the light. Although I lived a good and blessed life, I was still seeking to fill an empty space inside. I wasn't even sure what exactly I was asking for help with, but my internal suffering led me to the jungle of Costa Rica, and my help came in the way of becoming silent and still.

I can remember one particular night when all the jungle creatures began to sing their nocturnal melodies to me. A strange new feeling crept over my skin as I received their song. I took a deep breath in, becoming curious about the frequency I was feeling that lingered over me ever so softly. The "feeling" turned into a clear energetic vibration that began to expand and dance around me. What was this new sensation that tasted so foreign yet delicious to all my human senses? I surrendered to get to know what, or better yet, who was sending me such an irresistible invitation.

As I remained playfully curious, this frequency began to knock on the closed doors of my pores. I permitted my pores to open, and waves of vibrational light began to flicker into my body, floating around in my consciousness. My flesh merged with the light particles, and I was transported into a dark, empty space of gaseous plasma. As I rose higher into this vast dimensional plane, my pores blew wide open, and I felt the pressure of an intense light frequency wash through every single cell of my human body. It was a pulsating surge of electric, ecstatic bliss that fully consumed me. My body became a weightless buzzing rhythm that sounded like the constant purr of a delighted kitten. Curiosity conquered my feelings of fear, and I was like a little girl on Christmas morning, looking at the wrapped presents of the unknown that were screaming, "Open me!"

Each pulse of light energy expanded through my consciousness and quickly submerged me into the deep, spacious waters of Oneness with the "All That Is." The experience was beyond anything I had experienced in my thirty-two years of this human life. I was being held closer and loved more unconditionally than ever before. Any fear or resistance of allowing this vibration of light to take over me in any way it wanted had faded. My heart and buzzing body were becoming completely open to receiving what was being offered to me. And while my awareness caught another presence in the distance that appeared to be keeping watch, all the pieces of my fragmented awareness unified into the present moment in my Merkaba field.

I no longer tried to use reason or logic in an attempt to understand what was taking place. I just let go. I let God. In the precise moment when I reached the zero point of doubt and called upon faith to surrender to the Divine, my need for comprehension, understanding, or control completely dissolved. Grace gifted me total trust, which allowed me to be vulnerable, to embrace this unknown presence that was suddenly upon me. Complete confidence instantly created the space within to receive the orgasmic energy that permeated all parts of me physically, mentally, emotionally, and spiritually. A direct, energetic knowing had entered me; it was the spirit of Jesus Christ.

Growing up as a young girl attending Catholic school, I had, in fact, renounced my faith in Jesus Christ and was utterly disgusted with the seemingly impossible dogma of Christianity, yet here was His light and soul presence standing before my very eyes. The same omniscient alpha and omega light that poured through Jesus was now fully dominating me in my eagerness to be in total submission to the unconditional divine love He was offering. Jesus felt like a cellular, absolute divine knowing within my being, and I recognized Him instantly. Despite my prior rejection of Him, the feeling was so differently delicious— all I could do was say, "Yes!" to what was happening, and I allowed Christ to have his way with me in the Costa Rican jungle.

As Christ filled me with the unconditional love of All That Is, I joyfully felt the release of my many years of built-up tension toward Him that had resulted from mass social programming and conditioning. My soul and body were fully present and engaged with this quantum fucking of divine light and love as all the weary, ill thoughts I had been carrying—denying myself my own love and compassion—were rapidly bubbling to the surface.

As His tender yet strong, powerful masculine light continued to provide unlimited gifts of relief to every part of me, I opened myself to become even more vulnerable and receptive, allowing as much divinity as I could to continue pouring through me. I relished how He was just as hungry as I was to commune through this sovereign connection. He was committed to bring what was hiding in the dark into the light. No quantum fucking in the dark happening here; Jesus is an "all-lights-on" kind of guy. In my vulnerability, I began to witness all my past judgments, facing my own personal crucifixion that was displayed on a holographic big screen sitting directly in front of me. In an instant, He witnessed my suffering and graciously extended a quantum embrace, pouring forth a level of compassion I'd never felt before.

He anointed me with the power and courage of self-forgiveness, self-compassion, and self-honesty. This gave me eyes to see and ears to hear my inner truth that had been silenced by viral beliefs for decades. Jesus loved using the vibration of light and love to pulverize my past belief systems. The Master of Light never wavered in extending the utmost compassion as He continued this quantum fucking for my soul's highest good. I observed the viral strands unthreading themselves from my conscious and subconscious mind and biological DNA, then willingly merge back into the light strands of the supreme being's one and only true essence of love.

The ceaseless embrace of His fierce, rapturous, yet gentle divine love oozed waves of light over every strand of my DNA. I felt lighter and lighter as I was immersed in this unconditional love. He left no strand or nucleotide untouched. And just as a woman's pelvic floor softens to her lover's manhood, my entire essence felt loved and safe to open and soften to receiving more. My body's instincts as to what to do next came naturally. Just as the animal kingdom is blessed with trusting their instincts, my body instinctively prepared my mind to activate the dormant soil that was the foundation of my seed center. Miraculously, I had the divine, direct knowing that this was the ordained holy hour for the Holy Spirit to purify me from the thoughts, lies, and illusions I'd told myself my whole life until now. The hour was now upon me to flow pure thoughts through the river of my biological DNA, reflecting my true, divine nature so the dormant soil could prepare to receive the seed that was seeking to grow new life inside of me.

Christ was gently guiding me. He telepathically gestured to make sure I understood the truths He was about to instill that would atone for my false truths in a brand new way. This was the ordained holy hour to resurrect my inner light and truth. I immediately consented, remaining fully focused and attuned to the feelings of how humble and worthy I felt to receive this divine love. Rising to the same frequency level of this love and light was the only way I could fully receive the entire essence of what was, and has always been, available to me.

Ooh, yes! This was quantum orgasmic ecstasy on every level!

Every inch of me was being quenched as I bathed in His holy waters. A thirty-two-year spiritual thirst that had left me high and dry was now being quenched beyond my comprehension. Christ's divine presence was healing wounds I didn't even know

I had. I welcomed Him inside me. Desperately craving His full essence, I wanted and needed everything He was offering to my soul.

Following his guided invitation, I kept my thoughts aligned with the truth of the peace and love that is the totality of Divinity. I then gave my freewill permission to receive all of Him. I knew this was also a request for my rebirth and baptism by the true, pure light of Christ. As I asked to receive His entire grace, His frequency impregnated my spiritual womb. My sacred temple shook and quivered as all my chakras aligned. I was being blessed with the seed of Christ's light and love, and my whole body was in pure, ecstatic, orgasmic, indescribable bliss.

At the height of our climax, a shooting star appeared through my crown chakra and traveled down my pranic center, where it swirled throughout my heart and solar plexus chakras. Eagle feathers fanned above me, spiraling fragrances of frankincense and holy rose water over my helpless being, and I felt fully supported and cared for in every way while conceiving my new life. My Higher Self was delighted as She compassionately witnessed my surrender and acceptance of His invitation to receive this star as a new seed of light that traveled from my solar plexus, down to my sacral womb, and into my ovum.

Through the miraculous grace of God, the frequency of unconditional Christly love and peace was now a part of my DNA, consciousness, and etheric light body. My Higher Self was even more satisfied than my physical body after the seed of truth was planted. Pure, unconditional divine love and peace exploded through the grandest quantum love-making experience. Indeed, I was a child on Christmas morning, receiving the highest gift of communion with the one true presence who is simultaneously of form and formless. I was reborn with a new inner truth, returning to my eternal, divine essence.

My rebirth was complete. I lay there integrating this miracle as tears steadily streamed down my face. Innocence clothed my naked soul, keeping me focused upon the Holy One who was now awake and seeded within me. The once distant onlookers started to fade back into my third eye peripheral vision while I was in total awe of this new gift. My human body was glowing like a trillion stars from being fully cloaked in the indivisible innocence of love and light. Beams of light were pouring out of me as the resonance of perfect peace and perfect love. This was my new truth. This is who I Am, what I come from, and where I will return—perfect love and perfect peace—and it's the same for you and every soul.

Basking in the remembrance of my birthright and inheritance of peace, oneness, and unconditional love, the holographic images of my 3D timelines began to fade. As I watched them dissolve into the perfect and endless empty space of no-thing, I had nothing but joy, love, compassion, real understanding, and delight for it all—even for what I was once ashamed of. Foregoing the use of logical reasoning, I had fully reconciled with all my past transgressions and ill will against myself or others. I felt complete gratitude for every moment and lesson learned throughout my lifetimes. Any feelings of resentment had vanished, and all illusions of separation from God became a distant memory. With the winds of divine truth now blowing through my consciousness, I literally became a pillar of light. I was now intentionally and consciously pouring divine light from my cup, which runneth over with compassion, peace, and unconditional love into the cup of humanity.

As I lay there reborn, emitting light rays from my human body, the one ethereal onlooker became two, and with my permission, they both moved into my Merkaba field. I instantly knew who they were—Mother Mary and Mary Magdalene. My physical body was still vibrating from the intense, piercing heat of my baptism by the fire of the Holy Spirit. I felt like I was traveling at the speed of light. All sin—which I define as the temptation to turn against myself or feel separate from my Divinity—was erased. The fire of the Holy Spirit had purified me, and I had been seeded with a new conception of inner truth that would require careful nurturing.

The two Masters of divine feminine Christly light, Mother Mary and Mary Magdalene, each placed one of their hands on my light body and the other hand on my human body to assist in the seed being conceived in me. With their touch, I saw future moments of the sprouting that would take place from this new starseed within me that was shining as bright as the North Star. My seed would flourish into many branches with beautiful flowers that, in Divine time, would bear plentiful fruit, producing many more seeds to birth a new harvest of light. Yes, this was a beautiful tree of life, indeed.

Mother Mary and Mary Magdalene had been the keepers of the gate who created the safe space within consciousness and who built the bridge from the fast-moving light realm to the denser, slower-moving realm, creating a quantum biofeedback highway for the back-and-forth travel of my body to the collective consciousness of higher dimensions. They were there to make sure I would make a safe return, protected from any psychic attacks from a lower world suffering from viral programming.

The Masters of light helped to assimilate my stream of consciousness back to its Earthly home residing inside the sovereign temple of my human body. Now, plugging back into material form, I was still aware of and felt the electric current of Christ Consciousness. I had the direct understanding that both form and formless are equally sacred and to be treated as such. I was Divinity in human form, worthy of remembering my truth. And in my humanness, I felt as if I'd just dissolved into trillions of particles, trying to keep up with my consciousness which was traveling at the speed of light into another realm. My sweet, precious physical body that was a trustworthy companion on this sacred journey was tired. I was torn between honoring her request for rest and continuing this blessed quantum communion.

I prayed, "Please remain plugged into this new current of truth versus returning to the insanity of the viral untruths I once let live in me. Please help me hold onto this feeling and never lose this connection." I had a Divine knowing and understanding that I had already fallen from grace by unconsciously allowing the fear of loss, or the feeling that I could be separated, to reclaim residence within my thoughts.

"Motherfucker! Help!"

We all laughed.

No longer wanting to let the thought of loss or any other lies take back residence within me, I replugged into what Divinity was offering to be fully present in the moment. Three Masters of light were extending me an easy plug-in, and I didn't look away for the rest of the time I was consciously awake. I asked for their support in helping me to remember the truth that I am never separated from Divinity. I am One with it. I rested in the laps of these three Masters, feeling so grateful for their presence and guidance. The time had come to honor my body's request for rest. In an instant, I was back in the jungle, falling asleep under the Milky Way, listening to the melodies of mother nature.

Falling from Grace

Fast forward in linear time... I was fucked again, but not the good kind that happened in the jungle! Oh, how quickly we can fall from grace!

Damn you, Jesus! He fucked up my whole world! Shouldn't He have known and warned me how hard it would be to go back to my previous matrix of form, full of viral untruths, after being awakened to this new seed of truth? I had seen visions of its fruit...where were they? Didn't He know I hadn't learned how to harness the light to grow this light seed that had been planted? What a sick joke. Why didn't we talk about this in our quantum communion of love and light? How the hell was I supposed to go back to being joyful and fulfilled from being a top income earner who was receiving plenty of recognition and feeding the growing viral belief of self-importance from external validation? How could I go back to wearing all the fake masks after breathing in the truth of my true Divinity?

There are no words blissful enough to describe the communion made possible by grace, yet in no time, I found myself in suffering again. I was aware of this falsehood, but at times, I was suffering even more than I had before that fateful night in the jungle. I longed for that feeling again. I didn't even know it would ever be possible to harness that feeling again in human form, and it led to the external searching that never gives us quite what we're looking for.

The external search had me asking, "Come on, Jesus! Where the fuck are you now? I am looking for you everywhere, but you're nowhere to be found! With every church I go to and every time I try to stomach the book that has been used to box in your love, I seem to get further and further away from feeling your presence."

My inner truth was telling me, "You are not being silent, which makes you a perfect viral host." (Fear-based viral programming can attach itself to anyone who falls prey to things like scarcity, anxiety, anger, resentment, hatred, enslavement, greed, jealousy, revenge, shame, guilt, self-importance, judgment, seeking external validation, and more.) I ignored my inner truth, continuing to look for "that feeling" outside of myself, including in the bottom of countless wine bottles. Then one day, I just became tired of my own shit. Listening to the radio, I heard Brittney Spears singing directly to me: "You better work, bitch, you better work bitch." It was a message to stop being a victim and get to the inner work—lightwork, that is. So, that's exactly what I did. I'm not talking about effort-filled work. What I needed was to set aside daily time to sit in communion. I immersed myself in silent devotion, intentional breathwork, and journaling to high-frequency music for days on end. I spent as much time as I could in nature, giving gratitude for the elements. Inner Silence with my breath and nature's elements is where I was able to reconnect to His Christly presence. Jesus guided me to the book that led to the next quantum shift in my life, *The Sophia Code*, channeled and written by Kaia Ra.

The Sophia Code ® is a sacred channeled transmission featuring stories of some of history's most well-known Divine Feminine ascended masters: Isis, Hathor, Green Tara, Mother Mary, Mary Magdalene, Quan Yin, and White Buffalo Woman. It led to an upgraded path of self-mastery, teaching me how to surrender and use my free will to command my Higher Self to take over and operate my human consciousness instead of floating aimlessly in the collective consciousness that has been infected with viral programming and conditioning. I became fully committed to mastering my own internal connection and saving myself from the many years of suffering from alcohol overuse that I could not kick on my own. Within a year, my commitment to self-mastery, taught through the teachings of The Sophia Code®, delivered me from my suffering. My Higher Self led me to a method that I am fully committed to and on a mission to bless others with. I was shown that you cannot be fully present to your inner truth if you are enslaved to the overuse of alcohol. If you need assistance with this, please see my author bio section at the end of this chapter.

The Higher Self is one hundred percent immunized against viral programming and confusion. It has the sharp eagle eyesight of discernment to navigate you to the path of your highest good and it helps you keep on the straight and narrow path of your inner truth, even when surrounded by external falsehoods. The world is currently on its hands and knees, asking to be liberated from the enslavement of this viral programming. It has reached a tipping point because so many have shut off communication with their Higher Self for so long. Those awakening to their inner truth and Higher Self-connection are unifying around sovereignty and birthing a new Heaven on Earth paradigm. We use everything for our higher good and create our blissful lives, even if much of the world is living a life of hell on Earth.

The world of information and technology that is leading the viral programs of today is said to be here to "connect" us. I am sure you have had the following experiences:

You've been on the phone in an area where the connection signal is off. You can't make out the words of the other person you are trying to communicate with (communication, connection, and communion are interchangeable in many ways) and all you hear is static. You eventually hang up or lose the connection signal completely.

We have also gone through radio stations that go in and out, yielding constant static. Not being able to stand the static, we keep scanning until we reach a station that comes in with a better, uninterrupted connection. We then listen to the unmistakable sounds coming through and sing along with the familiar song that caught our attention in its familiarity and clarity. (Clarity around what next steps to take is always revealed once you get a strong connection.) Without a clear connection, we cannot hear our inner truth; we only pick up static.

Build a Clear Connection to Your Higher Self

There is only one pathway back to your inner truth to co-create a life of joy, bliss, and wild abundance to live each day in enthusiasm and with ease. That one pathway is inner personal communion with the Divine and your Higher Self, which are ultimately the same. This leads to honoring your natural, inner callings of interests, gifts, talents, and anything that evokes joy. No one can do this work for you; it's an internal job. In my inner communion and working with my mentors of the higher realms, I have discovered the treasures within our hearts are worth more than all the fame or fortune in the world. Our genuine interests of what makes us feel alive must expand and be acted upon to remain in alignment with our inner truth. Do not worry about goals, success, achievement, or money. (Read that sentence again.) What are your natural interests? What brings you true joy? If you spend time in communion, you will eventually become aware of what you are called to do and you will be inspired to get into action.

COVID-19 and the many global atrocities along with war consciousness have provided me with so many lessons, and humanity has called out to me for help.

I've been called to live fully in my inner truth. Humanity as a collective (which I am one with) is asking to be cleansed of viral programming and war consciousness. I am on a mission to be a pillar of light for this planet, harnessing and overflowing Christly light in my times of communion, just like that night in the jungle when pure light and love was gifted to me. I am a light worker who intends to be a lighthouse of miracles for humanity. The more I upgrade my light body, the more blessings pour out of me and into collective consciousness.

I recently birthed a new, unconventional church called Church of Sovereign Temples. Our mission is to assist humanity in awakening to its Sovereign Divinity through sacred inner communion. Our leaders and members offer support to those in need, thanks to our religious freedom in America. When my Higher Self led me to start this church, I questioned, "Who the hell am I to be a minister of a church, helping others honor their religious freedoms? I don't personally align with any organized religions, yet I'm supposed to start a church?" After sitting in communion and listening to the request from my heart, my soul answered with an enthusiastic "Yes!" Immediately, I flowed back into floating on the wings of joy because I was in alignment with the asking of my heart. By saying yes, I was honoring the truth of why I came to Earth, and all the moving pieces were effortlessly shown to me step by step within present moments.

We liberate the world when we liberate ourselves. Nations are healed when people are healed. Listening to and acting upon the inner truth of your heart is your greatest gift to humanity. Depending on your intention and how "wide awake" you want to be in knowing you are Divinity in form, you can begin to be in conscious communion with your eyes wide open. You can fully function in your day-to-day "reality" yet still be operating at higher frequencies. If you remain devoted to the ceaseless practice of inner communion, you will learn how to keep the communication lines open between you and Divine source, which are one and the same. You can be in two worlds at once. It is what I believe my friend and great Master of Light was trying to teach us to do when He said, "Be in this world but not of it." I am a devoted student of Jesus and many other Divine ascended masters. I am walking the path of becoming a Master of this method to fulfill my greatest potential in this lifetime.

When I asked my Higher Self to guide me in my most significant offering to you through this book, the answer was very clear. I invite you to learn how to work with your breath and engage in communion for direct connection into the stream of pure God-consciousness. Make it a top priority! If there is nothing else you take from my message, my heart beckons you to sit with this concept of inner communion and be willing to ask yourself how it can serve you.

Nothing ever came close to taking me to my inner truth in communions like the assistance from intentional breath work and use of natural elements as "medicine." Those, along with the sovereign teachings found in The Sophia Code®, are the alpha and omega tools to an inner awakening of truth and why I include them in my church ministry. They taught me a genuine inner connection, which my soul loved much more than "getting preached at" by others for salvation. We do not preach in our church. We have guided, collective inner communion, but we do not preach salvation. We are already saved and free! We are Divinity, formed in God's likeness. Starting a community like this required me to embrace my inner truth and shut out others' opinions entirely. Can you shut out all outside opinions and listen to what your heart is asking of you?

Trust that your Higher Self knows the exact right path for you and can help you use Divine discernment. This is how I awakened to reconnecting with and living out my inner truth.

Intention. Communion. Listen. Give gratitude. Allow. Repeat ceaselessly:

➣ I am willing to be an intentional breather and use my holy breath for purification from the Holy Spirit to receive my Higher Self more clearly.

➣ I am open to experiencing inner communion for my highest good.

➣ I am steadfast in my commitment to my direct path for commanding my Higher Self to operate my human consciousness for my highest good.

➣ I am awakening to my inner truth and allowing myself to receive my inner truth and digest it with ease and grace.

➣ I give my Higher Self permission to guide me to the exact next steps to activate and operate within me now fully.

With my free will permission, I command that all of this be so.

If these are sincere requests and you give your free will permission for your Higher Self to fulfill these requests, rest in peace and know that it is already done. And so it is. Amen.

May you go in peace. May you stay awake to your inner truth. And may you practice regular inner communion. And may you always remember you are perfect love and perfect peace.

I'll meet you in the garden.

"When you awaken to the truth within, you realize that there is just one moment. That moment is timeless because there is no other frame of reference for that moment."

~ Rajiv Agarwal

CHAPTER TWO

—◦◦◦—

A Nurse for the Soul

By Anne Henning

John Quincy Adams once said, "If your actions inspire others to dream more, learn more, do more, and become more, you are a leader." My life began as normal as anyone else's. I defined success and leadership through career and educational achievements as most people do. As I was a nursing supervisor and directed others, I considered myself a leader in the traditional sense. However, I was unaware of the powers of the Universe, let alone how to work with divine energy. Once I made this discovery, I began to realize my true leadership potential by demonstrating to others that we all can rise, expand, and create our reality. My story is not just about me; it is about all people who consider themselves to be 'normal' yet desire more out of life. I aspire to help others discover the Universe's powers that have enabled me to change my life. Those who seek to become 'more' often find that their transformed life helps those around them. In fact, by seeking to better yourself, you may be the one person it takes to reach another specific soul.

Through learning about energy, I understood that I create my reality. I no longer subscribe to old thought patterns such as 'life is hard' or 'I should be doing what others are doing to have a fun and fulfilling life.' Before realizing my actual value comes from my sheer existence, I wondered what the meaning of life was. I wrote it off as 'life just is.' I thought that, at best, we could try to be happy. My 'normal' world consisted of validation, expectations, and comparison. In the rat race, in the matrix, I continued through life in what society taught me to believe was reality. I saved money for the future so that I could be independent. I made intelligent and safe decisions like becoming a nurse, so I would always have a skill set and be employable. Before I knew it, I worked for a county hospital with the proverbial golden handcuffs. I felt trapped, even though others envied my life. Society's rules dictated that I keep my good-paying job with benefits; however, I didn't feel happy or fulfilled. I followed the rules, did as I was told, did not question the norm, and still longed for something more.

Working as an oncology nurse for 12 years, I rarely, if ever, saw a patient get better from their diagnosis. Most patients had no resources, no family support, and little motivation to get better. Fear consumed their auras. Nurses talked about death from cancer so frequently that when one brought her 3-year-old son to visit the hospital, he pointed to a dead cockroach on the floor and asked, "Cancer, Momma?"

Chemotherapy drugs and surgery were our patient's only sources of hope. A few years into my career, I gave up on thinking the billion-dollar drug industry could help my patients. Pharmaceutical drugs were band-aids for the root cause of the condition. Being immersed in my patient's purgatory of misery was my first awakening. A yearning to truly help my patients was steadily creeping in. It became apparent that I would need to break away from what is viewed as 'normal' in traditional Western medicine. I looked at therapies outside of what is typically prescribed in hospitals to see if alternatives held more promise. After researching a variety of alternative techniques, it seemed that the only thing that truly worked was altering the energy for a patient.

I vividly recall one patient who was healed from cancer. He was not the average patient. As a rowdy alcoholic, he required four-point leather restraints upon admission to help control his outbursts. For months, he stayed in our unit as he was weaned from the alcohol and received care from our hospital team. This hospital was a blessing for him as our community of loving nurses surrounded him each day. There were many jokes shared and lots of laughter during his stay. Research exists on the benefits of 'laugh therapy.' It has been shown to lead to cancer remission in patients (Tanay et al., 2014). The positive interactions led to good energy that helped him overcome his alcoholism and recover from cancer.

This patient's recovery due to a positive environment reminded me of a scientific study known as *Rat Park* (Gage and Sumnall, 2019). The research showed that when a drug-addicted rat was left in a cage alone, it would continue to choose the drug over water until it died. However, if a drug-addicted rat was placed in a community with other rats and had a nesting place, it not only avoided the drug, but the rat thrived.

Today, I am grateful that I see healing in a whole new light. I understand the power of energy alignment, balance, and harmonized frequencies. However, after more than a decade in medicine, I have come to believe that the most remarkable healing force is faith and love. It is said that faith can move mountains, and I have witnessed examples of dramatic shifts for the better that prove this.

In addition to my experiences in nursing, another catalyst for my mindset shift came from an Airbnb guest. She was a nurse in her sixties enjoying a cross-country adventure with a quest to see the natural beauty of the great outdoors. In a wise voice, she slowly said, "At a certain point, you look back and see you've lived half your life. You then ask yourself, "how do I want to live the other half?" This insightful comment prompted me to ponder what I wanted out of my life. First, I wondered, "Why am I not doing something I love?" Then, I began thinking of everything I hoped for out of life.

This new way of thinking correlated directly with my first monumental life path change. New supervisor roles opened across the hospital, and my co-workers encouraged me to apply. So, I did, and after being promoted, I found the position to be a much-needed change that I was unaware I needed. As a supervisor, I realized that I loved helping my nursing team become the best versions of themselves.

In this role, I was able to inspire, nurture, and promote change in ways I could not in a nursing role alone. To this day, I reflect on that special Airbnb guest and how that simple question prompted me to think about my hopes and dreams for life. I believe that this simple act of taking the time to ask questions on what would make me happy sent out my intentions to the Universe and forced my mind to find the answers that created my new reality.

I learned that the Universe takes care of the *how* on my journey. As author Marilyn Jenett preaches, "Forget the *how* and enjoy the *wow!*" Sometimes the *how* shows up in unexpected forms. One *how* came when I hit ground zero in my nursing career. The event that brought me to my knees and created a turning point in my life occurred in 2017. As a supervisor, I was also responsible for the duties of a charge nurse, which meant working a 12 plus hour shift on the floor with my staff. Days were getting rough; staffing was short, and workloads were heavy.

Simultaneously, our hospital was on a journey to achieve a prestigious designation called 'Pathways to Excellence.' As Chair of the Nurse Practice Council, I held a crucial role in supporting this objective. I dedicated myself to coming in multiple days in a row at various time slots, including 6 AM and 11 PM on the same day. Although I felt great value and achievement from all my efforts towards this shared goal, I was craving rest. A week passed, and my anticipation grew as I looked forward to the one day where I could come in at 10 AM and get a couple of extra hours of sleep. It was 5 AM when I answered the phone and was told, not asked, to come in and act as the charge nurse for the 6 AM day shift. This sent me into a state of complete despair and hopelessness.

As a 'normal' hardworking employee, I showed up to work. In the nonstop action of the morning, I dashed into the supply room, grabbing an item for a patient. I glanced over and saw our familiar supply room guy with his typical headphones doing his routine stocking. As I was multitasking, I said, "We also need more socks." He sarcastically said, "Good morning to you, too." Tears filled my eyes as I headed for the exit. The tears began to run down my face, asI ran to the privacy of my office.

I found myself crying uncontrollably as I entered the office. I left the lights off, and in the darkness, I slid down the inside of my office door. Landing on the tile ground, I curled up in the corner, where I cried between gasps of air. The last thing I needed was a sarcastic comment when I was already giving my all. In this moment of despair, I found that question again came to my mind: "Why am I not doing something I love?" and "How much longer can I do this?" The memory of my pain and tears serves as a reminder that I must *feel* to *heal*.

After this intense burnout, I could no longer see myself staying in bedside nursing. I was too drained to continue. So, to refuel myself, I began looking at weeklong self-help retreats. Yet something was telling me that a week alone was not going to be enough to recharge and rebalance me. Learning a variety of self-help tools was a start; however, consistently practicing the new habits would be the only way to sustain change. I decided to look for an extended program that would help solidify the transformation I was seeking.

The Universe listened to my request for a path to help me make the lasting changes I required. I was pointed in the direction of furthering my education, and I discovered a program in spiritual psychology. I would obtain a masters' degree while achieving personal life transformation with this plan. I felt a definitive calling to enroll in the program. This was my first step outside my 'normal' box. The course program consisted of healing the inner child, quantum energy work, and channeling spirit.

These topics resonate with my other interests, such as providing my staff with positive energy and pioneering integrative therapy modalities like Healing Touch and aromatherapy. I was ready to live outside the box; as living within its confines was not serving me. I was determined to get to the root cause of my issues and make real and lasting changes. I felt intrigued, excited, and inspired upon enrolling in the program! I dove into my nine-month-long journey towards a new lease on life!

On the first day of class in my spiritual master's program, I learned that all people are essentially love and joy. We are all divinely perfect. While we sometimes get distracted from our true essence by what society deems as 'normal,' we always have the option of returning to our authentic selves. Everything in the coursework embodied the underlying theme that love is the solution. My mindset shifted to the attitude: if I had to go to work, I might as well enjoy it. I took back things I learned each weekend and applied them to my staff. Each staff member I touched blossomed. Many felt safe to share their deepest pain. One shed tears of joy when she heard she was the definition of love, while another was unexpectedly relieved of the worst migraine of their life. I also connected patients with these modalities. Simple active listening techniques, holding space, and words of love created miracles.

I noticed significant changes by applying what I was learning to staff and patients alike. As nursing goes, some of the miracles came in the forms of unsightly bodily functions to finally arrive at healing. For example, a young 24-year-old woman was a patient battling leukemia for months. After I spent one hour with her, allowing her to unlock her self-love, her response was instant projectile vomiting, profuse sweating, and increased urine output. Her body was clearing the toxicities, both physically and emotionally. My experiences have taught me that the actual healing occurs through a complete mind-body-soul experience.

I've also learned that there is no 'wrong' method. Chemotherapy, diet, or laugh therapy are not sole answers; instead, the answer is the SOUL. Healing occurs when one believes in what they are doing. Adding awareness of intention, self-love, and forgiveness accelerates the healing process. The rules of the Universe began to restore my love of nursing and saved me. I learned that deep belief is an essential aspect of manifesting—not just health but any desire.

Manifestations were the next milestone in my new life path. My world changed remarkably after I took a course on abundance. Here I learned that I had to marry my conscious with my subconscious. My subconscious could not doubt my desire that my consciousness was speaking. Creating a neutral, positive statement allowed me to program my subconscious to believe that I already had it.

I first manifested freedom from the need to work. I was involved in many aspects of the hospital and loved by my staff. I didn't want to leave my team, but I also craved to be free from the need to clock into work. I thought about the other things I could do if I didn't have a full-time job. I didn't have the heart to quit, and I didn't want to get fired, but I wanted freedom. "Wouldn't it be nice if they asked me to leave and I could get paid?" is the question I specifically stated to the Universe.

I clearly remember the day walking from the main hospital to the building where meetings were held. I had a strong feeling that my role would be dissolved and that something better was in store for me. Before entering the conference, I looked up and asked the blue sky, "If leaving this position was what I wanted, why am I not more ecstatic?" The answer came in the form of a life-changing realization: my happiness does not come from my job. I create my happiness in whatever I'm doing. I felt an overwhelming sense of peace. I knew that whatever role I took, that happiness was within me.

The supervisor role was eliminated, and I decided to move back to bedside nursing. My staff embraced my decision to return to the floor with heavy hearts. It was going to be my first time as a night-shift nurse. My life force energy was starting to replenish. (I had time to eat, drink, and pee!) My former role as a supervisor was initially designed to be shared by THREE qualified nurses, which explains why I felt so overworked. I felt a trapped emotion of 'unsupported' in that previous role. Emotions are energy, and once I worked on my frequencies to clear 'unsupported,' my debilitating lower back pain spontaneously resolved.

30

Other positive changes resulted from the position change. I had much more free time. In this newfound freedom I started writing down my manifestations 25 times each day. I was using this technique to bridge the conscious and the subconscious. According to my program instructors, there are only two ways to change the subconscious: faith and repetition. Thanks to this repetition, the next big thing manifested.

The hospital offered a voluntary separation package for the first time in 20 years. I was ecstatic thinking of taking this offer and moving to Hawaii. Yet, I found myself deliberating with my ego about staying and playing it safe now that things were calmer. The going back and forth was driving me crazy. One day I just threw up my hands before I went into work and said, "Give me a sign that is so clear that I'll make my decision and won't change my mind!"

That night I went to work as a relief charge nurse. Working with my wonderful co-workers made the shift smooth despite an intense workload. A disagreement arose between me and an employee. The funny thing is, for the last 12 years, I thought to myself, *I could never work the night shift because I would never be able to tolerate the attitude of this person in inpatient placement.* None of my co-workers can remember seeing me mad or upset, but I was at a breaking point this night.

When the administrator joined the conversation, she told me, "Let's be professional." This was when I lost it. My years of accolades and awards were thrown in my face. They asked me a question and wanted me to check with the new manager I hired in the position I held just two weeks ago. I was so upset that I went to the tranquility room we had just opened in our unit, and I used it for its intended purpose. I cried, shook, and fought to catch my breath. Still shaken, I returned to the front nurse's station because my staff needed me as their charge nurse.

While walking down the hall, trying to regain my composure, I said, "I am so mad; I want to leave and never come back." Suddenly, it clicked. This was the sign that I asked for several hours ago. Laughter and relief flowed over my body. I happily went downstairs to my charge nurse meeting and then went around the corner to speak to the patient placement personnel. I apologized for my unprofessional behavior on the phone. With no apology forthcoming from her, I said, "Thank you." I do not think she quite knew what I was thanking her for, but I could not stop smiling the rest of the shift. That was officially the last day I ever worked at the hospital.

What followed next was nothing short of my childhood dreams coming true. Everyone in my family knew I always wanted to live in Hawaii, and with my severance package, I was free to go! I packed up all my personal belongings, rented my home fully furnished to perfect tenants, and with two suitcases in hand, I moved to Hawaii. The ocean view waiting for me each day was blissful! It also happened to be the ideal timing as my move to Hawaii coincided with the start of COVID-19 - something I could never have predicted. The Universe has an amazing way of managing the details. I believe that I was saved from more burnout at the hospital by leaving before the COVID-19 situation became omnipresent.

Looking back at how everything unfolded, I started to embrace believing, receiving, and trusting the Universe's magic. I know it works, even if sometimes you must be demanding. During my transition, there was one instance when I tried every which way to get something resolved. I even went to a therapist for assistance; they told me to journal about it. After parking my car, I angrily grabbed my journal, and I told the Universe, "If you don't show me the answer by the end of the day, I will lose all faith in you." That night at 9 PM, the answer was given to me in an easier way than I could have ever imagined. Another reminder that the Universe knows the how.

Almost two years into COVID-19, I sometimes ask myself, "Is it in my highest and best interest to go back to nursing?" My intuition always says no. I am still learning to listen to my intuition because my logical ego speaks so loudly. Yet, I will continue to listen to my intuition's advice. My calling is still to help others, really help others, get to the root of their concerns, and resolve them. I light up when I think of inspiring nurses to create their reality; however, that may look.

Reaching more nurses than just the ones I shared a hospital with is my grand vision. It was challenging to speak to nurses still on the floor for a while as some of them would break into tears, saying they couldn't take it anymore. They are grateful I made my escape and say it gives them hope. Although I left nursing, the burnout remnants have not fully left me. With nothing but island time and tranquility around me, I still find myself rushing as fast as humanly possible to make and inhale every meal. Each time I catch myself acting out this behavior, I allow it to serve as a reminder to slow down and embody my true joy being.

I created a transformation platform called I Choose Soul to help fulfill my mission to help other nurses and others burn out (www.Ichoosesoul.com). Here, services such as coaching and retreats are offered that utilize the Universe's beautiful powers to help those ready for change. I help my clients to become solution-aware instead of problem-aware. This mindset shift helps them to actively look for solutions. They are curious, intrigued, and want to know more. Several nursing clients with this mindset have become rejuvenated due to coming to my retreats and taking my courses. They see the value and the powerful solutions from taking action steps while looking within themselves for the answers.

Through the programs I offer, I have received immeasurable proof that the techniques work. I have seen social evidence, read countless testimonials, and heard glowing stories of client successes. The transformation has helped me learn how to guide people back to neutral and then forward towards their goals. Instilling knowledge and tools for clients' future use is rewarding.

I beam as I think of the first client I graduated. She booked a session just to tell me she was pregnant and how grateful she was not even able to put into words the changes she experienced. Waking up knowing I get to share my passions of teaching and creating excites me. I continue to become the best version of myself as I become free of the need for validation, expectations, and comparison. It has been a blessing to have found my tribe and a path that continues to spark my joy.

After completing the master's program in spirituality and graduating Valedictorian, I promised to keep learning and growing. This passion for education has occasionally led me down the rabbit hole of different healing modalities. For example, I recently discovered a Healy device that uses frequency to help align energy. One particular quote that resonates with me is from Albert Einstein, who said, "Future Medicine will be the Medicine of Frequencies." I can personally attest to physical ailments, such as my two-year battle with psoriasis, which resolved after only five sessions using this device. Currently, it is allowing me to have more courage and expand. All my fears and excuses are suddenly vanishing.

One example of how my fears have disappeared and been replaced by success involves a medical device my mother and I invented called The Beata Clasp. It seems crazy and almost sad that it took until now to unlock my ability to be in alignment with it. This product is fantastic. It organizes tubing, lines, and drains at the patient's bedside. I did one TikTok showcasing it, and it went viral with 1.5 million views. Nurses' comments were positive and encouraging.

This is another way I have stepped outside of 'normal.' My previous hospital declined to use the product even after nurses and patients trialed it and reported many benefits. Today, I am free from all energies that blocked blessings in the past, and we are now averaging one new hospital client per week!

When I zoom out, I see it is all a puzzle, and the pieces connect beautifully. The Universe itself is conspiring to get each of us to create and achieve all we desire. Magic is energy, and it is all around us. Yet, if we do not believe in it, we will never find it. Energy can be changed in a snap of a finger to whatever you want it to be. I promise you are just going through the steps until your chosen reality catches up with you; the Universe has a lot to adjust.

Every choice and action you make is correct. Give up judging your choices as right, wrong, good, or bad. Instead, practice forgiveness and give gratitude. My dad says my suggestion to write out his forgiveness was his life-changing moment. If I can break it down into a few things, it would be this: love is always the solution, you are already perfect, and remind yourself to be in the here and the now.

Simply looking down at our feet on the ground reminds us to be here in this moment. One story that always stands out is when a young boy in a tribe speaks to his grandmother. He observes that there are so many special ceremonies and rituals that their tribe celebrates. He asks her, "Because they all seem so important, which is the most sacred of them all?" The grandmother looked at the boy and said, "The birth of a child, so what does that make you?"

In my master's in a spiritual psychology course, my instructor pointed out that Jesus said, "The works that I do He will also do; and greater." I like to believe we are all God; we are all shared consciousness and a part of each other. Life is meant to seem a little chaotic as the Universe experiences itself in infinite ways. The most positive impact from my journey was simply that I moved towards my joyful self. I will keep raising my vibration, which inspires those around me.

We, as humans, have the power to amplify the vibration of gratitude. Imagine the awe of the beauty you experience sitting on a hill and watching the sunrise or sunset; that is the energy vibration we give off to give back to this planet. It is what makes humans so unique. What is the only difference humans will have from artificial intelligence in the future? We can love. When you cannot give love, simply take the route of trying to understand the other person.

Each day I am reminded of the quote by Erma Bombeck, which reads, "When I stand before God at the end of my life, I will hope that I would not have a single bit of talent left, and could say, 'I used everything you gave me.'"

I was normal; I still am normal - only I have found 'more' by finding joy and happiness in my everyday tasks. I have now redefined 'normal' for myself as having a loving and joyful human experience on this Earth. I believe part of my destiny here on this planet is to have discovered my soul's calling for divine learning and finding peace within myself. Gratitude for my new mindset to create my reality allows for infinite possibilities. Universe, thank you for giving me the gift of my 'new normal.' It enables me to fulfill John Quincy Adams's definition of leadership as I inspire others to "dream more, learn more, do more, and become more."

I wish you the best on your journey towards inner and outer leadership, and may you find the peace, joy, and love within you that your soul is destined for.

Citations

Gage, S. H., & Sumnall, H. R. (2019). Rat Park: How a rat paradise changed the narrative of addiction. *Addiction*, *114*(5), 917-922.

Tanay, M. A., Wiseman, T., Roberts, J., & Ream, E. (2014). A time to weep and a time to laugh: humor in the nurse-patient relationship in an adult cancer setting. *Supportive Care in Cancer*, *22*(5), 1295-1301.

"To become learned, each day add something.
To become enlighten, each day drop something."

~ LaoTzu

CHAPTER THREE

From Trials to Truth

By Andrew Geldert

PART 1: Living the Life of Mistruth

Bang, bang, bang, bang, bang, bang...

Six shots rang out above the pumping techno music. Moments before I had been standing at the bar of my local nightclub, arm in arm with my best mate, having the time of our lives. I was 25 years old, a testosterone-fuelled bull, an alpha male I liked to think, full of ego and living life in the fast lane of partying and recreational drugs. I was a free spirit but I was also desperately seeking parts of me I felt were missing, and I could not seem to shake the feeling of being angry all the time. Many years into my future, at the perfect time and after much self-induced suffering, I would realize that I had become the product of my broken past, shaped into this form by witnessing things that no kid should ever have to see. When I reflect on my life journey, I can draw upon a feeling that was always pulling me towards a greater understanding of myself and the world around me. I was seeking my inner truth, and there was no place I wouldn't travel in this quest to find myself. I now understand very clearly why the journey unfolded as it did for me, as every situation I would face played a significant role in shaping me into the man I am today: connected, open, fulfilled, and living out my soul's journey through my passionate purpose of generating value in the lives of others, putting back the things I took away over many years.

But back then, I knew none of this – I was still stumbling through the dark. I used my professional training as a boxer to my advantage. I projected my anger into the world at every opportunity I was given, especially by other men who were bigger than me and thought they were tougher than they really were. My attitude and lifestyle led me to seek a brotherhood, and I found comfort in the arms of an outlaw motorcycle club. During my school years, I never really had any mates; as I got older, the mates I did have, became like my family and the code was loyalty at any cost. This night would test that loyalty to its very core as I witnessed my mate become involved in a brawl with an opposing outlaw motorcycle club's associate. My commitment to his defense would almost cost me my life.

I'm not sure to this day what kicked off the brawl, but an attempt by the other group to outnumber my friend called me to action. As I entered the fray, the man I made my advance towards stepped backward, fumbled around his belt line, and retrieved a handgun. Rather than run, I held my ground and challenged him to use it by holding my hands out and waving him on. When he did nothing, I called what I thought was his bluff and stepped toward him, going into attack mode. Rather than fight me, he emptied the gun, I gave him no choice. The music was replaced by the screams of women as people in the crowd ran feverishly toward the exit. When he began firing, the distance between us was no more than two meters. I saw very clearly a flash from the chamber, immediately followed by a sharp pain, as if someone had driven a sword through my chest. I hunched forward as I struggled for breath. Shock quickly set in as I too became part of the crowd, bumped and shoved as I staggered to the exit where the bouncers stood directing people out of the doorway and into the relative safety of the main street. I told one of them that I had been shot and needed an ambulance, then laid down near the front desk. Within a few minutes I was lying in a pool of my own blood; I looked down to assess the damage. Lifting my shirt up, I saw blood spurting and bubbling from a bullet wound high in my chest. Passing in and out of consciousness, I was fighting to hold on until the ambulance arrived, I felt cold. I had been in the army, operating as a reconnaissance/sniper soldier, and my training enabled me to recognize that blood bubbling from the wound was the sign of a punctured lung. I rolled onto my side, so the punctured lung was closest to the ground. This way, my good lung would not fill with blood and cause me to drown before the ambulance could get to me. I did feel death, it was closing in and the place I went to one of peace and tranquility, but I knew it was not my time.

I later discovered that I had also been shot through my trapezius, the muscle that joins the shoulder to the neck. Two bullets, had they been a few inches closer, would have resulted in one shot through my heart and another through my jugular vein. I had been extremely lucky. I spent two weeks fighting for my life in Intensive Care, waiting for my lung and pierced liver to heal. My mate was shot in the stomach, and an innocent female nightclub patron was hit in the back of the neck by a stray bullet that ricocheted off a cement pillar. As I lay there, I knew it was not my time to die. Even as I drifted in and out of consciousness, my soul was choosing life; I knew I had much to live for, and my search for the truth was underway.

PART 2: The Breeding Grounds of a Deluded Truth

I never quite knew why, but I always felt different from everybody around me, and I never fit in throughout my school days. Always on the outskirts of groups, I found myself just wandering around. I used to make it look like I was going somewhere so that no one would realize I was walking around lonely and by myself. My reports were always the same. They said, 'He shows great potential but fails to use it.' I was always a shorter kid but could never understand why I was bullied at school and in football training.

At the age of seven, my parents broke up and my beautiful mum went looking for love in all the wrong places. After a few years, we ended up with no money and lived in government-supplied housing, scraping by with minimal food and provisions. As a young man, I witnessed something that, when I look back, would alter my life's journey significantly, forcing my down a long, dark and lonely road. In the same small town, we would move some eleven times in as many years. One of those homes was a tiny three-bedroom, one-bathroom house, a home so small that one could hear every word that was spoken from the opposite end. At the time Mum was in a relationship with a very broken, violent, and alcoholic man. He used to come home from the pub and they would fight. I could hear her whimpers, and everything that was happening to her.

I was frightened of this man. He once beat my brother and I with a kettle cord folded in two for having a pillow fight when we were supposed to be sleeping. Not being able to save my mum from this man made me feel very weak. This emotion would soon manifest as anger and a vendetta against men in general. This particular evening, my life as an 11-year-old boy would change forever. A fight broke out between them, and I heard my mum scream that she wished he would go and kill himself. He stormed through the house, slamming the back door. I watched out of my bedroom window; the back yard lit up by a street light just outside our back fence. This enabled me to see him clearly as he entered the shed, came back out, scaled the woodpile under a large ghost gum tree, tied a piece of rope around a large, low-hanging branch, then the other end around his neck, and stepped off the woodpile, his body swinging limp in the air. I screamed to Mum, ran through to the kitchen, grabbed a knife that turned out to be blunt, raced up the woodpile and began feverishly hacking at the rope. After what seemed like an eternity of listening to mum screaming as she attempted to lift him up and take the pressure off his neck, he dropped to the ground. He survived, and to my surprise they stayed together for a few more years after that.

Not long after this event we ended up moving house and for a while, things got a little better. As for me, personally, life was about to begin to spiral out of control. One afternoon I came home from school with a swollen face. I had been punched by one of the older boys after school, and when my mum's partner asked me what happened and why I did not defend myself, I told him I did not know how to. His response was to put me in the car and take me down to the local boxing gym. I stood back as he spoke with the coach and from that day on, I was taken under their wing. I became very passionate about boxing.

I improved quickly and started to beat the better boxers in my age group. I took my new skills to school and began fighting with anyone who wanted to pick on me. I felt standing up for myself was changing people's perception of me. I liked the new-found respect I was being shown and the confidence boxing was giving me. At the age of 11, I had my first fight in the boxing ring at the State Novice Titles. Boxing also gave me an outlet for the internal anger that was simmering beneath the surface. I found an increasing number of reasons to project my anger, and the release was something I grew to rely upon. I was also a talented Australian Rules Football player. At sixteen, I was invited to play professional football, but my temper and Mum's drive to keep me focused on school overrode that opportunity.

PART 3: The Search for the Truth Begins

I left school in Year 11 because my grades had taken a dive. My drinking, partying and fighting continued to be an issue for me. I started work in my first job as a landscaping laborer, and before long I could not deny that I was living a dead-end existence, as the cycle of work, drink, partying and fighting wore me down. I began seeking a way out, and when I saw an advertisement for the Australian Defence Force, I had a light bulb moment. Within a few months, I had applied and been accepted.

In the early days in my Army journey, even though I was almost kicked out for fighting during my training, I achieved a great deal of success, receiving an award for Best Recruit - Skill at Arms for my weapons handling and accuracy, and the award for Best Trainee Soldier at Physical Training, which for me felt amazing because we were pushed extremely hard and I was up against many fit and strong candidates. After I completed my training, I was posted to the 2nd Battalion Royal Australian Regiment (2RAR) to begin my journey as an infantry soldier. I continued achieving high-performance levels, making the battalion obstacle course team, ranked in the top ten in the battalion's military skills competition out of 500 soldiers, and was selected for the Dog Squad as one of seven soldiers to compete on behalf of the Battalion at the Australian Army Military Skills Competition. I was also chosen to attend two of the top training courses in the battalion – the reconnaissance course and sniper training. In the second year of my service, I was transferred out of my regular platoon and across to the recon/sniper platoon with an aspiration to try out for the SAS – that was until our battalion was placed in lockdown and on short notice to leave for East Timor. Within a week were shipped out of Australia to what we were told was a war-like situation, to conduct border operations in remote areas on the East and West Timor border. These were intense situations, ceasing and arresting Indonesian militia and conducting raids on militia strongholds in the Timor region. As a recon/sniper platoon, we were the spearhead for all primary operations in the initial stages of the occupation.

Upon return from active duty, my commitment and enthusiasm to be part of the military wavered, along with my aspirations to join the SAS. In my mind, I had achieved everything I set out to accomplish, aside from becoming part of the SAS. But more to the point, I had an intensifying issue with authority. The more the Army tried to control me, the more out of control I became. My disillusionment with the Army made the idea of returning home more and more attractive, so I set my sights on a new horizon. I had searched the Army for my truth, and I found pieces of it, but I still had a long way to go.

Leaving the Army within months of returning from East Timor, having operated in such an intense situation, we were left feeling wound up like a spring that was ready to let fly. I know this may be hard to comprehend, but not actually being directly involved in war, or carrying out what we were trained to do, specifically firing our weapons, took more of a toll than anyone who did not experience the situation could understand. There was no release of the built-up tension. I am not saying that killing the enemy would have been a better outcome, but the anxiety of walking on the edge the entire four-month deployment was a burden we did not fully appreciate at the time. This was compounded by the fact we had very little debrief upon returning home, instead, we were just expected to carry on as usual. We had no idea of the demons we would face as the reality of our service began to rear its ugly head in the years to come. To me, it comes as no surprise that East Timor has the highest rate of suicide of any Australian deployment.

PART 4: The Great Awakening

Feeling like I had achieved everything I set out to achieve in the Army, my search for a deeper truth called me back home. Little did I know that a vacuum awaited me. Without the structure of the Army, before long I was sucked into the life of a free spirit, reveling in my newfound freedom, and the cycle began; partying, drinking, taking recreational drugs, and fighting continued to repeat itself. The money I had saved during my Army service ran out quickly and I began dealing party drugs to facilitate my lifestyle. My behavior quickly came to the attention of the local ruling outlaw motorcycle club. I started off fighting against them, but soon fell in with them as my desire to be part of a brotherhood beckoned. During the tumultuous years to follow, I would be shot twice in the barroom brawl, become a nominee member of one of the staunchest motorcycle clubs in Australia, and later, become embroiled in a six-month undercover joint Police Operation between the Gang Crime and Major Crime Squads, and be subsequently charged with dealing commercial quantities of cocaine and sentenced to seven years of imprisonment for my involvement in an international drug syndicate. At the time of being arrested, I was riding high. I was 31, at the peak of my influence. I was wealthy and living a life of luxury and notoriety. But being charged and sentenced was about to turn my life on its head, and for my good.

The first six months of my sentence were spent in a maximum-security prison with some of the worst criminals one could imagine. I once sat next to a man who lured two young women into his car and brutally murdered them both. One look at him and you could see he was a very dark human being. This time in maximum security made me want to do the rest of my time as easily as possible. After proving my focus was doing my time and not presenting any management issues to the prison hierarchy, I was fortunate enough to be classified as a minimum-security prisoner. Soon after, I was shipped to a prison farm. It was like being transported from hell to paradise, a concrete jungle to a country retreat. It was this place, nestled in among gum-tree bushlands, old-growth rose bush gardens and heritage-listed buildings, that the veil of falsehood about who I was dropped. No longer could I run from the man in the mirror. In the coming years I would face so many profound truths, as the reality of my situation dawned upon me in proper.

I became more inspired to seek the truth of who I had become than ever. I was ready to begin taking full responsibility for my actions and the behaviors that led me to hurt myself, my family, loved ones and the victims of my crimes. I did not blame or deflect, I stepped into full accountability; the time had come to own my mistakes. After accepting responsibility, I then moved into a period of repentance. I was sorry for my wrongdoings, and in being sorry I laid the foundation for forgiveness and reconciliation. Reconciliation for me was recognizing the broken pieces of myself and the influence my childhood was having upon me as an adult. Having recognized my own brokenness I chose to begin the process of restitution, and that was putting the broken pieces of myself back together and healing my brokenness. I deeply embraced the meaning of forgiveness; forgiving myself and all those that had hurt me, or who contributed to my brokenness. I was lucky enough to be a participant in a course that exposed prisoners to victims of crime. I will never forget listening to an elderly couple tell the story of how their son was brutally stabbed to death by a man on drugs. I was struck with emotion at seeing and hearing their pain. It dawned on me that my decision to sell drugs could have contributed to a crime such as this. I was awakening to a new truth and I was struck by the significance of the revelations I was having.

Every day I set new intentions and more demanding challenges for myself. Recognizing that I was ego-driven, I strived to teach myself humility. Rather than stand at the front of the food line and defend this position with my life, I waited at the back of the line until everyone had eaten. Lo and behold, when I reached the front of the line there was more food and less guilt at loading my plate up. I was last to eat but gifted with more food than being the first; this was profound to me. Early in my sentence I thought I was too good to contribute to my community of peers by scrubbing the continually filthy bathrooms, even though it was my scheduled day. Now I began cleaning them with more effort than I would clean my own toilets at home! I took my personal development so far as to conduct conversations without swearing or slandering, talking negatively, or engaging in dialogue that was not conducive to my growth and development. I failed so many times that I questioned if I was setting myself up for failure or just driving myself crazy. Self-doubt crept in and I wondered if I was ever going to succeed, but not once did I give up. It became obvious that I was holding onto a lot of past traumas that I had buried deep within me. I chose to confront the fear of talking about what I had seen and been through by communicating my inner demons to some beautiful people I got to know extremely well in the prison chaplains, Mark and John, to me they became the guides on my journey back into light. I could never thank them enough for the influence they had upon me. Making myself vulnerable and breaking the fear of talking about my past, was a significant catalyst to my transformation. I felt the weight of the world shift from my shoulders.

In the years leading up to being charged and sentenced, I owned a trucking and earthmoving business. I was always an entrepreneur plagued by delusions of grandeur. I enjoyed being a leader and business manager but knew I did not have the technical or interpersonal skills to be the best I could be as a business leader.

A stipulation relating to having the privilege of being housed at a minimum-security prison facility was that offenders had to have a job within the prison. There were work-parties that would go into the community to do general maintenance tasks or internal work-parties that contributed to the daily running of the facility. I chose neither but opted to study fulltime, which was fortunately considered a job. I set my goal to complete a university degree. I completed a Diploma of Project Management in a matter of months then signed up to study a Bachelor of Business with a major in Human Performance Management and a minor in Business Management and Leadership.

My daily routine became two hours a day of physical training and included being the captain of the prison football team. This was a real privilege as we were released each weekend to play in the local league where our families were able to come and visit us; for a day we got to feel 'semi-normal.' Eight to ten hours of my day was devoted to studying for my degree (two units per semester for four semesters per year or eight units in total), a few hours to personal development study and an hour to play the guitar and sing, which was something I always wanted to do but never had the time. I attacked each day with renewed enthusiasm, using every last minute to achieve maximum productivity, value and benefit from each moment. My mindset changed from prison being a bad thing, to being the best thing that had ever happened to me. Here I was, on a farm and in nature, recalibrating my sense of self, investing all that I was into who I wanted to become, creating a new reality for myself. My crowning realization was that I was sent to prison to become a free man. I was in exactly the right place to grow and become the best version of myself that I could be. I was being blessed and the truth was being revealed to me. I embraced this journey with all that I was.

PART 5: Inspired to Live My Truth

I completed my Bachelor of Business with a distinction grade average and completed two more diplomas. In the final six months of my sentence, I was lucky enough to secure a work-release position with a global logistics company as a warehouse assistant. I was trained on the forklift and loading trucks with freight. Every day I turned up, I worked like I was working for my own company. If I was asked to sweep the floor – and I was plenty of times – I swept the entire floor as clean as it had ever been. One of the lowly jobs in the warehouse was the pallet yard; it was never cleared of pallets. I cleared every pallet, swept the yard, and asked for more work when I was done. Upon my release from prison, I was promoted into the office. While employed there, I gave the role my all, but I was now a free man after five years, and greater things were calling me. A good friend landed me a role in a mining services company as a project supervisor, fly in fly out, on better money than I had seen for a long time. Soon enough, I was promoted to project manager and was running multi-million-dollar contracts for some of the largest mining companies in the world. And still greater things were calling. After 18 months in the role, I had saved a deposit and went looking to invest in a business that would see me at home every day. I had spent enough time away from my long-term partner and kids as it was and after all I was an entrepreneur not an employee.

I went looking and found a construction business for sale and negotiated an up-front payment and the remainder of the $500,000 acquisition on vendor-financed terms. The business degree served me well as I facilitated most of the transaction and due diligence myself. In 12 months, my business partner and I had grown revenue from $1,000,000 to be on track for $7,000,000. But the growth came at a cost; I was working 16-hour days, under an enormous amount of stress, and as it turned out, we had taken on too much overhead debt and the business did not have the level of clientele as the previous owner had represented for the purposes of the sale. To facilitate the amount of debt we took on to get into business, we needed to win larger contracts and more of them. In the end, we did not win enough work, and our margins did not realize enough profitability to keep the business afloat. A hard decision had to be made, so we entered the company into voluntary administration.

When I took the news of the company failure back to my partner of 18 years, it was the final time I would defy her opinion. She had never supported me leaving the security of my $180,000-a-year project management role, or buying the construction business, and so, she broke up with me. I left the house that night after breaking the kids' hearts with the news of our separation. They were 12 and 8 years old at the time. I took with me just a bag of clothes and a broken heart. I had failed my relationship for a second time, and also in my attempt, to build a multi-million-dollar business empire.

PART 6: The Truth Revealed

My vision of climbing to the top of the corporate world and being inspired to achieve my fullest potential, had resulted in me attaching my sense of self-worth to the outcome of the businesses and reaching the financial success I had set out to achieve. Here I was, suffering, down and out, broke and broken-hearted, facing a new set of truths. By this time, I was conditioned to adversity and I knew that this was just another set of circumstances that would somehow benefit me in the future. A new reality dawned and I welcomed it with open arms and an open heart. I was on the flip side of being the managing director of my own construction company, having come so close to building something I dreamed of. Yet towards the end, even as I prayed for that miracle contract that never came, I could not help but feel both my relationship and the business were stripped from me for a greater purpose.

Despite the hurt I was feeling, I was as committed as ever to the next phase of the journey of seeking the truth of who I was and my purpose in this life. I had discovered that the corporate world did not satisfy me as I thought it would. Upon reflection, I was not happy, and I realized that my self-worth was not contingent upon the business and or monetary success. Seeking the deeper meaning of my destitute situation, I followed a calling that I could no longer deny. The calling was for me to use all of my life experiences to help others. I felt I had a lot to give so I embarked on more study in fields of life, transformational, personal and relationships coaching, and also studied human energy and how it affects our mindset and life. I achieved related accreditations in Reiki, Tantra, and Hypnotherapy. I never looked back. I launched my new business and brand, backed myself in, and took myself to the market. The outcome was a level of success that I never thought possible. I had clients booking in within days of advertising. My soul's journey towards the revelation of my truest identity I felt was complete.

The satisfaction I got from coaching was overwhelming and watching people reach their goals deeply satisfied me. I had come full circle and after all my struggles, I was now operating in the capacity of giving back and there was no greater feeling. I was in service, replacing the things I took away by leveraging my healing journey, failures, successes, and life experience. I started a men's online support group called the Man-to-Man Brotherhood Movement, which now has almost 700 members, and a media company signed me to develop my own men's mental health and well-being podcast series called 'Man to Man – Let's Talk About It.' My entrepreneurial journey morphed into my becoming involved with three different companies, for two of which I became the global business development manager, leading the capital raising effort to fund their projects. I was recently a finalist for the most inspirational man of the year at the Mates in Construction – Men in Black Ball 2021, and have been a guest keynote speaker at various engagements, talking with both youth and adult audiences about the power of human change and overcoming adversity.

PART 7: Living My Inner Truth

Layer by layer, situation by situation, my inner truth was revealed to me. Yes, I was seeking this truth, but more importantly, there was no other way to find myself, to discover my truth, than the way I did. Each situation I used for my good, with the perspective that nothing is happening *to* me but everything *for* me. I am not proud of my mistakes, nor do I want to glorify or minimize my wrongs. Every person, every soul, has a journey to undertake in this lifetime, each unique, none less or greater than another's. I have chosen healing and forgiveness, to become the best version of myself in this life, to live my truth, and release my deepest soul's journey. I cannot tell you how many fears I had to embrace along the way. Letting go of what was to welcome what is to come and become fully present, to be the light, the pure love energy that lies within each of us, I claimed this with my entire being. One cannot fill an already full cup, I embraced the process of emptying my cup, seeking my cup to be filled with love by reconnecting with the love of myself and in turn others.

My journey has led me to finally realize the truth of who I am; a divine creation, unique and wonderful, a miracle, born and given consciousness by the Universe for it to observe its own beauty, and this you are too. So, drop the lies and illusions and adopt your inner truth. And I hear you ask, but how do I seek my inner truth? To begin, go deep into silence, deep within your YOU-IN-VERSE, and there you will find the still small voice inside of you, the one you have been programmed to shut down, the one that holds your most authentic identity – a more powerful and creative force than you have ever known, that awaits you to be heard, followed, acted upon and lived out, for you to be inspired by. Take that time and find your inner truth. This is the ultimate souls' journey of every human being, and it's never too late!

Here is my inner truth spoken, for the first time:

'I come in peace, with a message of hope and healing for the planet, a message of love and truth so powerful that the world will alter its future.'

In the perfect timing, I will be given the voice to speak this message, beginning with a TED Talk sometime this year. And will continue with my dream to have a movie concept I wrote called 'The Perfect World,' an epic tale of how this beautiful but broken world heals itself, made and produced into a block buster movie.

As for the rest of my awakening and journey of inner truth, it is, as it is for all of us, a continual work in progress. One that I embrace each and every moment while I am blessed with this wonderous gift called LIFE…

"The spiritual journey is the un-learning of fear and the acceptance of love."

~ Marianne Williamson

CHAPTER FOUR

Seeking Support & Activating Allies

By Angela Orora Medway-Smith

Cariad Spiritual

The Practical Mystic

I'm Angela Orora, a spiritual channel, teacher and author, Life & Soul Alignment Coach and retreat leader from Wales, UK.

When I wrote this chapter, I felt a huge responsibility because truth and honesty are important. I've looked back through events in my six decades on this planet to find points where a connection with my soul and inner truth was awakened. How support and guidance from my spirit guides, guardians and allies have flowed, weaving the path to enable and empower me to follow my soul's purpose.

My inner truth is my connection to the very core of my being, and I'd like to share with you how this alignment helps me live completely in ease and grace, no longer resisting my soul's path.

"It's so frustrating!" I told my husband, *"My guides are clear. They want me to teach. I've booked the venue scheduled 22 classes, but when I sit down at the computer to complete the lesson plan, I get nothing! It's been a week and I still don't know where*

to start. I'm going to take a day off tomorrow and maybe go to Leslie's meditation group. See if that helps."

He nodded in support without looking away from the television. *"Sounds like a plan."*

It had been two years since I gave up my job in education and started my spiritual business. My business had evolved from working as an energy healer and clairvoyant locally, to organizing charity festivals, fayres, and spiritual events. To then making the 400 mile round trip to London fortnightly to work as a spiritual consultant at Mysteries, the world-famous esoteric book shop in London's Covent Garden.

After over twenty years of marriage, my husband was incredibly supportive and used to tell me to follow my intuition and 'go with the flow.' Our son had moved to London and working there meant I could see him regularly; our daughter was at college with plans of heading off to university in the autumn, which meant I had ample time for my spiritual work.

The following morning, I headed out to the local community center set in the middle of a leafy park. I stopped for a moment, breathed deeply, listened to the stream tinkling gently nearby. The birds serenaded me as I headed into the red brick building.

A circle of chairs was laid out in front of a table adorned with candles and crystals. The smell of incense hung in the air. I smiled from the heart; I loved Leslie's circles. They were so welcoming. Laughter rang from the kitchen. I dropped my coat and bag on a chair and headed in to join the group.

The routine was the same every week: a guided meditation, a short break and then some mediumship or psychic development.

Most of the lovely ladies who came didn't really need the practice; it was just a place to gather with friends. I didn't come very often but was usually led here when I needed to listen for a message.

So, it wasn't a big surprise when close to the end of the morning, one of the ladies said, *"Angela, your grandfather is here, he has a message for you."* She went on to describe my grandfather, a gentle giant of a man who rarely stepped back into this world unless it was essential to support me. *"He says, step away from the computer, what you need is on the bookshelf,"* she continued excitedly, *"and soon your training courses will have accreditation, you'll be teaching all over the world! He's very proud of what you're going to achieve,"* she said with a beaming smile.

I thanked her and smiled in disbelief. Even though I'm a medium and had received a clear message, I had doubts. *"How can what I need already be done? My home is filled with bookshelves. Would I need to look through every book? There's absolutely no chance I'd be putting myself through accrediting my courses, WAY too much work!"* I puzzled, *"My grandfather had taken the trouble to bring me the message, so I should take a look, at the very least."*

An hour later, I was opening a dusty envelope that had miraculously found its way to the bookshelf in my living room. Inside was a typed, photocopied lesson plan for a 22-week intuitive development course. The envelope and its contents had been given to me thirty years earlier by my spiritual teacher, the wonderful Betty Balcombe. I'd taught it when I lived in Sydney in 1990. I have no idea how it came to be on that shelf. I'd moved homes three times and every other book on the shelf was under ten years old!

I firmly believe that if our soul's plan includes something we need to do, we will be provided with the means to do it. Our spirit guides and ancestors are there to assist us.

I taught my Intuitive & Spiritual Development Course in person four times. First, my students learned and practiced psychometry (reading photographs or objects). Then, during the sixth week, they'd be challenged, reading photos inside sealed envelopes to show them how much they'd developed.

"Write some notes and tell me what you've picked up," I said to my Tuesday morning class. We moved around the room one-by-one as the students described colors, shapes, feelings, and images they'd picked up holding the sealed envelopes. Only to open them in amazement and find they'd tuned into the energy of a place or person, picked up the color of clothing, the shape of a mountain or the bends of a river on the pictures inside.

"I've drawn a picture," said Ann, *"the more I tune in, the stronger it gets. It's as if I'm watching a video. I'm seeing a young woman in a dark robe holding a chalice. She's a Priestess, I think? She's with a small entourage and I can see the pyramids. They're in Egypt".*

"What do you feel?" I asked.

"A deep sense of service, of contentment," she answered.

"Okay, let's open the envelope. You may have picked up on the past life of one of the people in the picture," I said.

Ann opened the envelope and my jaw literally hit the floor as she pulled out a school photograph of me, aged seven. She handed me the drawing, *"You need to keep this and ask your guides why they're showing you this."* she smiled.

Later, at home, I sat in meditation with sacred oils. I'd just started Myrrophore work, the practice of meditating with individual oils to learn from them, tuning into their sacred vibrations. Some brought forward ancient symbols, some images and messages. I hadn't worked with Myrtle before but had been guided to select it.

I inhaled the scent deeply, closed my eyes and relaxed. The smell brought more smells forward. Sounds and images started to play as I was transported back to the same life that Ann had seen earlier.

"Lie down and relax, sister. I'll fetch us some water," I said, as my companion made herself comfortable on a lumpy-looking mattress on a low wooden bed. I looked around the sparsely furnished room. It was hot and dusty. We were both heavily pregnant, plaster peeled off the walls and I could see the brickwork underneath.

I shuffled to the next room, where men huddled on stools around a wooden table. I was handed a clay jug and a drinking vessel and returned to my friend, who smiled at me as we drank thirstily. My name was Mary, and my companion was Mary Magdalene. We were in Egypt. The image faded.

"What does this mean? Why am I being shown this? I don't understand." I quizzed my guides.

"Follow the signs and listen," said a voice. Not a voice I recognized. *"A new guide perhaps?"*

Later that same day, I was checking my e-mails when my phone froze. Unable to scroll back or forward, I paid attention to the message. The College of Psychic Studies in London was running a workshop four days later: "Receive the Keys of the Pyramid," it read.

I turned to my husband. *"Darling, I'm going to London on Friday. There's a course I need to be in."*

The initiations I received during that workshop changed me and awoke my ability to channel Ascended Masters and Angels. As a result, the Ascended Master, St. Germain became a regular visitor to my development group. My connection to my guides and higher self (my soul) became crystal clear.

Our higher self, guides, and guardians will create opportunities for our learning when we need them, using whatever means available. Therefore, listening and following these signs, omens, portents, and messages is important.

I continued teaching, moving my focus to teaching healing. *"The world needs healers to help with what will come,"* my guides said.

I'm passionate about healing! I first qualified as a healer in 1985. I wanted to awaken others to the benefits of holistic therapy. So, I started holistic festivals and fayres in my town, raising money for local baby and children's charities and giving a platform to some excellent holistic therapists, artisans, and mediums.

It was at the Summer Festival that one lovely medium said, *"Angela, you will write a book and it will be called The Book of Many Colours."* I smiled and thought, *"Here we go again! I really have no idea what this is about. I have no wish to write a book but tell me how and I'll get it done."*

My guides continued, *"You need to gather these five people together and you will be shown."* Pictures of the people that spirit had selected flashed before me. I knew some very well. Others were acquaintances. Two were at the festival that day.

I approached the first person, a lady I'd met once when invited to speak at a local Theosophical Society meeting. *"Do you mind if we chat?"* I asked, leading her toward the side of the room. I continued, *"Apparently, we have some work to do together... there will be six of us, and I know it's a project for St. Germain and that's all I know at the moment. So, what do you think?"* Her answer was a resounding *"Yes!"* The same answer came from the remainder of the group, and we met a week later with no real idea why, except that each person had a deep sense of knowing that the task was really important.

So began my preparation and training to be a clear channel for the Ascended Master and Archangelic Collective. To learn, allow my consciousness to lean aside and let my physical body be a tool for these beings of light to communicate with humankind.

It started with holding St. Germain's energy for a few minutes before my blood sugar levels dropped and I needed a break. Finally, after a few weeks, I could hold his energy for an hour. The other Masters and Angels followed: Mother Mary, Lady Nada, Lady Portia, Lord Kuthumi, Archangel Haniel and others. Before long, I'd negotiated my boundaries, was aware of my physical limitations, the mechanics of moving in and out of light trance mediumship and was able to be a clear channel.

The restrictions imposed by the pandemic in 2020 did not hold us back. The channelings continued with different Ascended Masters and Archangels making their voices heard. They gave personal messages to my healing students as I shifted to working online.

I was invited to the Caribbean and Italy to work at retreat centers by people who had heard about my work.

"I can't possibly go," I told my husband, nervous about the potential travel restrictions.

"What's stopping you? If you think you'll be safe, then go!" he said.

"Well, nothing... I'll meditate on it and go from there," I replied. The answer was a resounding yes.

Traveling in the early months of the pandemic was a terrifying experience! Four weeks later, I was being herded into line at Santo Domingo airport arrivals by the army, dressed in full PPE and carrying guns. It was like being in a scene in a dystopian science fiction film. Children were crying; people shuffled about nervously as we were lined up against the walls having our blood taken and tested for COVID-19. Then, slowly, we were herded to another area awaiting the result before clearing customs.

I finally emerged into the hot tropical night for the five-hour drive through several police curfew stops to the very end of the road at the Samana Peninsula.

In this unspoiled natural paradise, the clarity of my task and the channeling of *The Book of Many Colours* began. I stayed in a little wooden hut in a glorious tropical garden, next to the turquoise waters and pristine beaches of the Caribbean Sea. We had clear blue skies filled with black Sea Eagles.

The peace and tranquility enabled me to slip effortlessly into a trance.

St. Germain began, *"The material you will write about is already known to mankind but is inaccessible to most and out of date.*

Since 2012, your planet has changed in vibration and the divine energies that are now accessible to humanity have changed. Therefore, these teachings need to be simplified and made available to humankind to assist with their ascension and understanding of their individual soul's paths. You will pass on this message to them."

"Are you ready?" he asked, *"This is your time – the time of enlightenment. You can choose whether to sit, remain in your current position and be blind to the possibilities, or embrace them. As always, it is your choice. The balance of existing in this human world or soaring with all the gifts of your spirit are your choices.*

"Choose wisely, dear one. Your future and indeed the future of all sentient beings depend on this choice. So, where do we begin with your instruction? The information you will find on these pages is not new. My brothers and sisters have delivered it through many channels, many times. You will find it presented here in a simplified fashion – as needed at this time – for it to be accessible to humanity as a whole in this new age. Your planet is fragile and so is your species, so many gifts have been bestowed upon you that have gone unused, wasted, or exploited. However, it is not too late; indeed, it is NOW that is the time to become fully awake, to utilize these gifts for the benefit of ALL."

NOW I understand!

I'd already learned that humanity now had access to twenty-eight divine rays, rather than simply the seven written about by the great channels: Helena Blavatsky, Alice Bailey, Godfre Ray King and others in the 19th and 20th Centuries. The Patrons of these Rays, drawn from the Ascended Master and Angelic Collectives, wanted people to connect with them so that they could guide, inspire, and enlighten them. But this connection needed to be simplified!

I'm a practical person. So, I set about thinking of sensible and straightforward ways to present this information so that even an absolute beginner could understand their soul's path, awaken to their inner truth, and begin to live their life in grace and flow.

Showing people how to work out which of the Divine Rays their soul had decided to incarnate under would be the key and then explaining who and how to connect with these unique beings of light.

How I wished this information had been available to me when I'd begun my spiritual exploration in the early 1980s! We as humans weren't ready and the energy wasn't accessible at this time. I became incredibly excited about how this information could simplify complex esoteric teaching and awaken people to their inner truth and their soul's purpose.

And so it began, the channeling of *The Book of Many Colours; Awaken Your Soul's Path With The Divine Rays*." I was sent a book coach when my human mind felt the book wasn't good enough. A publisher when I faltered and an *accidental* set of Oracle and Affirmation Cards when my illustrator misunderstood one of my messages and produced them in glorious color in one day. Finally, this little book was published on 11.11.21, meeting St Germain's schedule!

Tapping into these incredible energies can provide you with unlimited support to help you be more intuitive, more creative, receive healing, motivation, unconditional love, or nurturing energy, create your miracles, awaken to your inner truth, and align with your soul's path. In addition, you can find out which vibration, which Ascended Master or Archangel, can support YOU on your personal soul's path! The Divine Rays are the keys to this and much more.

You see, awakening to your inner truth is not complicated. You don't have to spend years on spiritual study, train in mediumship, or spend hours and hours in prayer.

We are all divine beings having a human experience, sparks of the divine in human form, Gods or Goddesses, each capable of creating miracles, of moving mountains.

All that is needed to awaken to your inner truth is an understanding of who you are. To create an intent to align with Divine Rays and your spiritual team in meditation and then follow a simple process. It's as easy as 1, 2, 3.

> ➤ Making the time to create a connection
> ➤ Genuinely listening and watching for the signs and portents
> ➤ Following the guidance

Our lessons can't all be theoretical; they need to be practical. The choices and mistakes we make, just as much as the good decisions and the relationships we choose to experience, all bring us closer to our inner truth.

It's also essential that you recognize your OWN truth and understand that everyone has their perspective. It's absolutely critical that you are discerning. No individual, particularly a spiritual teacher, should tell you that theirs is the *only truth* and that what feels right to you is wrong. Their truth belongs to them, and you should find your own. It should feel right to you on an intuitive or soul level.

Awakening to your inner truth is *just* the beginning. In my experience, the next thing that you need to do is learn to trust and follow this guidance; only then will your life begin to flow with ease and grace.

I spent years ignoring, arguing, and challenging guidance. We are human, none of us is perfect and that's okay. I see this life like school, and we travel through kindergarten through university before we return home to our soul.

So much support and guidance are available to us from our support team in spirit and the Patrons of the Divine Rays. Developing a relationship with these beings of light brings transformation for us. It impacts the planetary collective consciousness. Very simply because we raise our unique vibration as we transform, and this effect ripples out. You may have heard this concept called The Butterfly Effect. This is not simply a spiritual concept, even Einstein talked about Quantum Entanglement and how we are all connected. How, when one thing happens in the universe, it affects all other things too.

Much of the work I do these days is based around the Divine Rays. Helping awaken divine souls like you to their power and potential. I have found them an incredible resource for personal and spiritual development and personal and planetary healing. I hope that you will find inspiration and support from the Divine Rays, Sacred Fires and their Patrons, the only limitation is your intention!

"Awakening to the truth is a deep realization of what you are as an experience. What is it that is listening? What is it that is feeling? Feel it. Sense it. Welcome it."

~ Adyashanti

CHAPTER FIVE

―――――⊸o⌒⌒o⊸―――――

When My Heart Cracked Open

By Helle Lisle

Istill remember the morning when my heart cracked wide
open and I had no other choice but to fully surrender to what
I later realized was my inner truth and my connection to The
Universe.

That morning, as always, I kissed my husband goodbye. It was a
beautiful summer's morning and I loved the fact that I had a quiet
two hours before work. I made myself a cup of my favorite coffee as I enjoyed the view of the flowers blossoming in the garden. I smiled and felt gratitude in my heart – felt so blessed.
Then suddenly I felt this well-known heavy sensation in my
chest and I became aware of a feeling of sadness. I knew that
sensation so well – it had been a recurring guest, since I had collapsed with severe burn-out symptoms in 2014.

Sorrow of "the life I had lost" – the loss of identity, of the person
I used to be and of the ability to be more active both physically
and mentally. Unlike the first years after burning out, I was now
able to welcome the emotions and just accept them visiting me.
Knowing that they would pass again, leaving me stronger and
wiser.

I grabbed my coffee and went outside, walking barefooted in the
freshly mowed grass. Appreciating our green and lush valley, I
sat down smelling the coffee and feeling the sun on my face.

"It's ok – I'm ok ", I whispered to myself, just accepting the sadness – embracing it – being still. I felt my heart open and I just surrendered to everything that was.

Suddenly, this great light beamed towards me from The Universe. A divine vibrating light filled with love. The light and the vibrating energy filled up every cell of my body and at the same time surrounded me. I felt held and embraced by it.

I had never experienced anything like it before.

Then the words came flowing from The Universe. They were so simple but an overwhelming truth: "You are love and awareness. You are already unconditionally loved. You are already whole and perfect."

The message felt true and nothing in me questioned it. I felt the energy and vibration of the words magically landing in my heart. They were repeated again and again, almost like a chanted mantra, flowing from The Universe and into my heart and body – as a sensed experience of light and love.

My heart recognized the message right away. The words resonated with an inner truth my heart already knew. I felt no doubt, no resistance and no fear – I felt more awake and present than ever before. A deep feeling of bliss and love filled my heart, body and mind. Witnessing how my heart cracked wide open and feeling this gratitude for life beyond words, I felt my soul awakening and unfolding. I intuitively knew that the message from The Universe carried my truth.

I felt myself surrendering to this magical moment and to this message from The Universe. I felt completely whole and more connected to this source than ever before. I felt one with the love and the light. A feeling of bliss and ultimate freedom filled up my heart and my body.

For a moment, the words stopped and I just sat there, more awake and alive than ever before.

Then the light and the words from The Universe returned: "Now spread this message. The message that we are all love and awareness. That we are loved unconditionally. That life on earth is given to us as a precious gift". The message flowed towards me, carried by high vibrating energy and an immense beaming light.

Then everything went quiet. I felt the sun on my face and looked around the garden where everything was back to normal. Just as it had been before this magical experience. But inside of me, everything was changed. I had a profound feeling of being in contact with deep inner peace, joy and love.

It isn't easy to put this amazing experience into words. When I try, some of the magic disappears. I hope, however, that you get a sense of my moment of "awakening to my inner truth".

This profound experience took place in June 2018 and has changed my life.

I collapsed with burnout symptoms

Let me take you back to 2014. I was living a meaningful and busy life with my husband and two boys in a small town in Denmark. For around ten years, I ran my own psychiatric practice and really enjoyed my work. My focus was on helping clients primarily using therapy, mindfulness and compassion rather than just prescribing medicine.

One day, as I was sitting in my clinic at the end of my workday, I found myself sobbing and feeling completely exhausted. It was a cold and rainy day, already dark outside. I felt pain all over my body and so tired that I could barely move. My mind was a total blank. Then, after a while, I heard my inner voice saying: "I can't keep on living like this". That day I collapsed with severe burnout symptoms and I haven't worked in my clinic since.

The ever- increasing bureaucracy made it difficult for me to do my work the way I wanted to. The endless red tape made it so I had less time available for working with clients in a meaningful and respectful manner. The way I had to do my work got more and more out of alignment with my values and my approach to clients. I was continually confronted with clients stuck in the health system, witnessing how this aggravated their situation and mental condition.

During my sick leave, it came as a shock to me how burned-out I was. Even though, when I look back, all the warning signs had been there for a long, long time. For years my body had tried to wake me up, telling me that my life was too stressful and increasingly out of alignment with my true purpose.

There were signs and physical signals that all wasn't well throughout those years. Although I was aware of these, I kept postponing taking action. I always thought that I would feel better when ...! I did not realize how close to the edge I was.

Consequently, I ended up in a terrible state until finally, I had no choice but to give up the life I knew. At that point, my condition was so disabling that I was nonfunctional in my work as well as in my personal life.

Burnout and chronic fatigue had been professional areas of interest to me as a psychiatrist and now I felt all of these disabling symptoms in my own body and mind.

I remember how just going for a short walk would deplete my energy entirely and leave me nauseous, dizzy, with flu-like symptoms. I felt exhausted and had to remain still for the rest of the day.

I had a long journey ahead of me. I struggled to find true acceptance of my situation. Unconsciously, I carried on trying to use my old strategies to get me out of that harrowing situation. Pushing myself, struggling, fighting my symptoms, not respecting the signals from my body. I wasn't showing myself enough compassion and self-care. I had started a new business working with private clients, running groups where I taught mindfulness and compassion. Although, I now had the freedom to decide how much I wanted to work and what kind of work I wanted to do, it was too much. Most of the time I was still in survival mode.

Looking back, I was still living according to old paradigms, belief systems and my old mindset. Without realizing it, I hadn't made the profound changes necessary to start healing.

One of the things that made the situation especially hard was the shame. I was an experienced psychiatrist, teaching mindfulness and compassion focused therapy, working with many burnout and chronic fatigue clients. Still, I collapsed with severe stress symptoms.

"How could this happen? I should know better", that inner voice told me. So even though I understood why I had ended up with severe burnout symptoms at a conscious level, my old limiting beliefs kept on working in my subconscious mind.

The voice of my heart

Then one day, at the beginning of 2018, I had a profound experience. It was another cold day in Denmark, and I was resting on my couch as so often before. I had just completed my morning meditation and felt at peace and fully present. I loved these mornings alone in our house with no set agenda for the day. I looked at the fire burning in the woodstove and felt surrounded by warmth.

Suddenly, I felt someone sitting next to me on the couch. A loving presence of some kind delivered this message: "Stop fighting and trust that everything will be fine". The moment was brief, but I felt connected to a wise and loving source. The experience left me with a profound feeling of knowing my way out of my painful situation.

I realized that this was the voice of my wise heart. This was my inner loving voice which had tried to get my attention for such a long time. Unfortunately, for years, I had been too busy and too stressed to acknowledge it. Previously, when I'd heard a similar whisper, I had ignored it and failed to realize how important its message was.

That day in 2018, for the first time, I fully accepted my situation without resistance. With that came the profound knowledge that life would again be ok. That I would be ok. Looking back now, I see how fully accepting my situation rather that resisting it, released energy.

Throughout my years with burnout and before, I had been doing inner work through meditation, reflection and mindfulness practice. I'd become increasingly aware that my mindset and beliefs were sabotaging my healing process. I went on retreats to work with compassion, self-acceptance and self-love.

However, before this profound experience of really connecting to the voice of my heart, part of me still hadn't entirely accepted the depth of change necessary for me to begin the healing.

From that day everything started to fall into place, not all at once, but day by day I experienced my life changing for the better.

In June 2018 I had the magical experience of my inner truth fully awakening.

The first thing I had to change was getting enough rest to renew my energy rather that keep pushing myself. By forcing myself to continue working at the same pace, depleted my energy even more. It is still surprising how much rest I needed to recharge my inner energy battery.

I had known this to be true for my clients but accepting that this was now also true for myself took a long time for me. In a way, it was such a simple change to make but still so very difficult to include in my practice.

Learning to respond in a loving and caring way to my need of rest taught me how powerful the programming in my subconscious mind really was. I would find myself sitting on the couch with my embroidery, having decided to rest, and the next thing I knew, I was cleaning the bathroom. My most stubborn old belief to let go of was that prioritizing my own needs was equal to being lazy and selfish.

I had to learn to give myself "permission" to put my own needs before the needs of others and before the tasks on my to-do-list. Habitually failing to prioritize my own needs over others and the demands of everyday life, was a significant factor in me burning out.

I was always a resilient and energetic person. It had never previously been an issue for me. However, failing to renew my energy levels - physically, mentally and at a deeper soul level - eventually left me completely drained of energy.

Even writing this now, knowing how important it is to acknowledge and respect my own needs, my old self is still trying to pull me back onto my old path. Awareness of what energizes, inspires and makes me happy is, to this day, something that needs my full attention.

An important lesson learnt was committing myself, and my limited energy, to my healing process and not letting other things come first.

I often used this mantra during this time: "May my mind be peaceful and may my heart be open". This helped anchor me to a new attitude towards myself and life in general.

I find gratitude to be an inner super-power, for clients and for myself. Through gratitude, I connect to my inner source of joy, love and peace.

Looking at life through the lens of gratitude changes everything.

It helps me remember that life is full of miracles. It opens my mind, senses and heart to the magic around me. A beautiful sunset painting the sky in fabulous colors. The beauty of a flower. The heartwarming feeling of my son's hand in mine. Looking into the eyes of a loved one.

I became one with my inner truth

The magical experience in June 2018, where my heart cracked open and I became one with my inner truth, was the beginning of my true transformation.

From that day on, I allowed myself to listen to my inner truth rather than constantly overruling it. I stopped letting my mind and ego define my next steps forward.

I started to truly listen to the voice of my heart. The message was clear: It was time to let go of old habits, old limiting beliefs, old stories as well as old thoughts and emotions. All those things kept me stuck in a reality that I didn't want. Facing that fact was painful and debilitating for me.

I had consciously known part of this truth for a long time, but that day this realization became a part of me in a way that led me onto a path of change.

Fully embracing that I was already whole and loved unconditionally, I felt free, joyful and completely at peace. I felt deeply connected to both my own essence and to The Universe.

Through my study of the work of HeartMath Institute and visionary people like Joe Dispenza, Marci Shimoff, Eckhart Tolle and other spiritual teachers, I have found a way of relating to life and to myself that feels completely aligned with the true version of me. It has been like coming home. An inner knowing that my true path will unfold step by step as long as I stay awake with an open heart.

This new knowledge has bridged the gap between the scientific and the spiritual view for me. It connects the dots and enables me to believe wholeheartedly in this, my new paradigm.

Through this work, I have realized how we can co-create our life with The Universe, especially when we can fully trust our own full potential.

Fast-forwarding to today. I'm now in a place where I feel well and love my life. I've changed my business so that the work I do aligns with my soul's purpose. My work inspires me and ignites that inner joy.

I have learned to trust and honor the voice of my inner truth and the voice of my heart. My heart is the seed of my soul and is connected to the wisest and most loving part of me. The last few years have taught me to trust and surrender to the flow of life. It gave me a deeply felt knowledge that everything is going to be ok and that I am already whole and loved.

This doesn't mean that my life is without challenges and painful experiences. Those are all part of human life. What has changed is my attitude towards what happens in my life. I am able to look for opportunities and learn lessons in confidence, knowing that The Universe always has my back.

I still get frustrated, impatient or sad. But even when circumstances are difficult, I try to stay aware and connected to my heart. I try to let go of the need to work things out, to fight and attempt to control reality. Of course, I don't always succeed, but I listen to the signals of my body and heart. Then I make the necessary changes when I feel out of alignment. Sometimes I can do this straight away and other times it takes me a while.

When I connect to my heart again it becomes easier for me to stop fighting what is already happening. When I find myself accepting and surrendering to the present moment as it is, I find peace and happiness.

Even though I had some difficult and painful years following my collapse with burnout in 2014, I now believe they were a gift given to allow growth and expansion of awareness and love for life.

Today, I know we can all learn to trust our inner truth. To see the essence of who we truly are. Trusting in the voice of our hearts and making decisions aligned with our essence changes everything.

Peace, joy, love and freedom are freely available when we connect to our inner source. We are divine beings with infinite potential and co-creators of our own life. Trusting in this and in The Universe makes all the difference in the way we live.

When we understand that we are not our past. We are not the stories in our minds. We are not our own limiting beliefs. We are not our old habits. We are free to create the life we dreamed of and to love life.

"Being at ease with not knowing is crucial for answers to come to you."

~ Eckhart Tole

CHAPTER SIX

—◇○⟨⟨∽⟩⟩○◇—

I Met Me

By Grit Sanders

"All sorrows can be borne if you can put them into a story."

Karen Blixen

"THERE HAS BEEN a shift last night," the voice continues. "Listen to the messages." I listen to the uplifting words conveyed with great seriousness. The voice coming from my inner self sounds familiar. It's lucent and elegant and like my regular voice. As I turn around, my face carefully snuggles into the soft pillow, creating a shadow from the dim light of the wall lamp. It is still very early. Almost numb from the mesmerizing sleep that still clings firmly to the pictures, "Write it all down," I hear. I smile pleased. So much has happened since the first touch of my awakening nine years ago.

I TRY TO SQUEEZE the skin on my upper arm; nevertheless, I feel nothing. Like frostbite, stunned by self-medication, I shut-down my emotions, leaving a body only to view life in black and white. The riverbank is busy with exotic pictures. I am holding my much-loved antique Hasselblad camera, and my pockets are filled with Kodak color films in crackling orange foil, but the craving has completely gone. The excitement and desire that had kept me afloat and been my bright momentum for the last six months have evaporated. Instead, there is a sum of voices around me. Water splashes widely from women hitting the wet, twisted clothes against the riverbank. An activity of murky water from the riverbed surrounds the drowsy cows grunting contentedly, merging with frothy shampoo well rubbed into the toddlers' carbon black hair. The sun is warm with a golden glow we only experience at sunset in Denmark. Suppose we are lucky enough, that is. The heat embraces me lovingly. I pinch my skin harder this time but feel nothing. Absolutely nothing.

I had not slept since Monday, only three days ago, when my husband chose to tell me he wanted a divorce. It wasn't a surprise. Blinded, we have been living together for quite some time not noticing each other, like supporting roles—in the background without any dialogue. It was so empty. I felt so empty. Facing back-to-backI had quietly cried myself to sleep for a year. The mutual gratitude and romance had slowly diminished, just like our friendship. The sorrow lay a heavyweight on my shoulders, forcing them down and forward, closing my heart a little bit every day. Still, it was devastating when he made the choice. I felt I had to amputate a part of myself. We had been together since high school. I did not know how to be me without him. The fear of being alone was my worst enemy. The thought alone felt suffocating. He ended our twenty-three years together with a text and a letter. Secretly, he had left the house with a suitcase and did not return. Was I alone in this marriage? Did he not respect me enough to look into my eyes? All the questions made my head spin.

I recall my childhood, the slight soft tone calling out for me. The voice comes from within, maybe from my unconscious mind or the universe. It entices single words like Calling, Soul, Love, Meaningfulness, Purpose. Like tiny seeds gently lifting from the dandelion, resting on the wind until it's time to germinate. At night they are luminescent. They never sleep. The words are stored inside me, just like the most important key events, until I am ready to face them. Everything has a beginning, but am I ready?

Lying contradicts everything I stand for. When I left for India, I looked my children in the eyes and did not tell them the truth, as if everything was fine. It cut me like a Swiss army knife. I had left the little village and my house crying, but it felt necessary to complete the trip. I was determined, hoping it was all just a nightmare I would soon wake up from.

Everything and nothing had happened in just a few days. Thousands of kilometers away, I am now contemplating the river of Ganges, surrounding Varanasi, the holiest city of Hinduism and host of the many pilgrims. The boat I am being transported by is no bigger than a spacious rowing boat with room for me, my luggage, and the men I have hired to freight me from the main road outside the city. As I approached Varanasi, a massive crowd of men welcomed me by shouting at each other while their bare upper bodies struggled to flush the huge masses of mud away from the riverbank. The challenging annual rain season had just ended and left what used to be the bottom of the river. The sticky, orange, wet masses covering the stairs slowly made their way back towards the river as I jumped over the boat railing with flip-flops and folded trousers.

The city rose hours ago. Smoke from the many cremations along the river lies like a dense blanket between the low houses. Small, winding, narrow alleys are busy with a constant crowd of people trading while gesturing hands dance together. Cow manure is left to dry on variegated railings before being used as insulation on the flimsy roofs, the dry, dusty air amplified by running squeaking children. A scent of deep roasted spices of the east does its best to tone down the tarty smoke from the corpses that nibbles my nose.

The many men wrapped in sarongs as skirts are still working diligently to spade the last layer of the sticky soil away. Slowly, the big tiles become more visible, showing how I can walk along the water, looking for exciting faces. I love faces, different versatile faces, or just faces that tell me the first sentence in a story where my curiosity is captured. Walking for a while at a leisurely pace, my thoughts lead me back to Denmark and my disappointment in myself.

For as long as I can remember, it has been my greatest desire to be a mother, be happily married, be surrounded by our families, and have quite a large circle of friends. On top of that, I even had a creative job as a children's clothes designer in a partnership company with my best friend.

Now that I think of it, it sounds radically naive. But the fact is that this is how we lived for many years. Everything came true. We were blessed with three beautiful children, fun and inventive. Nothing was missing in my fairytale. I had been happy all along, right up until the cracks began to show their claws. The lonelier I became, the more I began to shut down my feelings, the more hysterical and impossible I became.

Poor sleep and constant pain from tension over my lower back began to erase what was left of me. After way too many hours of working late at night, stress became my enemy. Small businesses with colorful clothing, which magnetically occupied many stores in several countries, suffered from a lack of my frozen creativity. I had to stop and deprive my dearest friend of her job when we chose to sell the business. A self-hatred went from embers to fire, and I distanced myself from what I thought I knew was me.

Right up until my eyes caught an older man waving his hand, making signs to summon me, I taste nothingness. I have no idea how long I have been walking around in my own thoughts, feeling I am neither in Denmark nor India.

I look to both sides. Is it me he is waving at? I look him in the eyes. He nods gently. Curiously, I walk towards the mature man sitting on a *Gather*, a stone staircase leading downhill to the water, which the pilgrims like to use. His reverent open palms welcome me to sit close next to him. Somehow his gentle dark brown eyes communicate I am safe here. The orange turban tightly tied around his head and a colorful mark on his forehead steal the attention from his white robe and the many pendants with beads hanging around his neck. A long, light gray curly beard that, with a smooth transition, becomes lighter in length emphasizes his character of wisdom and a grandfather-like warmth. The large gray stones on the stairs are warm, clean and inviting.

I wonder what he wants of me. I am puzzled and drawn to an atmosphere, an inner peace that is beginning to take form despite all the hustle that is going around. Without speaking the same language or even trying to communicate with a sparse number of words and drawings by hand, we sit like this, close to each other in the space of calmness.

Like a great mute button is being held down, my thoughts remain quiet, and an emphasis of silence almost engulfs the sounds swirling around us. As we sit like this for a long time, absolutely nothing is present besides the two of us. I close my eyes and inhale deeply as all my control gently evaporates and my muscles melt to softness.

Surprisingly, I observe an energy wave rushing through my body with currents of bright light. As if I had been thrown into the deep water with a chain around my ankles and was fighting my way up to the surface, my mouth immediately instinctively draws in the air again. Gasping to breathe.

"What happened?" I ask without a voice.

"You have been healed," not knowing if the voice is telepathy or my intuition speaking.

The man is sitting completely still.

"Can this be?" I answer back.

I've never tried healing before, nor do I know anything about it. It just never had drawn my attention. But now, as I sit here breathing once again with the blood pulsating through my veins, feeling my skin gently under the white, loose, blonde blouse and khaki shorts, I am blown away in awe. It is a very physical, living, and present experience.

We are still sitting close to each other but with enough space for the holy man to have a cloth bag between us. I have not really noticed it until now. It looks like any other Indian fabric bag, as lightly dingy gray sack with stains from some sort of dried liquid. The opening is pulled tightly together with a string. Baba, as I call him, gently lifts the bag and opens it slowly, almost caressing his cloth and pulling out a snake. A smaller one approximately a meter, he smoothly places in my hands. The lukewarm and dry scales feel soft against my palms. A beautiful, unique pattern that runs along the back with brown- and cream-colored shades slightly moves in slow, mesmerizing strokes. I don't even know if I am breathing right now.

I'm sitting here with a snake in my hands. Me, who always have been so afraid of snakes and trembles by the mere thought of them. Why am I so steady? This unusual inner calmness is by no means recognizable. But I enjoy feeling empowering me.

Baba takes out another snake he is happy to sit with. A third snake peeks out on its own, exploring the narrow space between us. The man clearly has great affection for his animals, showing them respect and humility. His gentle energy rubs off on me. I love everything about this experience. It is as if he knows exactly what challenge my soul is going through at this time of my life and what I need so much. Again, I feel a vital, euphoric, high on life.

The healing is much more than a quiet moment that brings the opportunity to breathe again. It is more like a kind of initiation of a spirituality in which I do not understand the meaning of yet. Like a shooting star has brought me back to life. I now recognize the magical well-known colors and scent of spices swirling around me, just as I remember from my last trip to Kerala earlier this year. The India I fell in love with.

Nothing short of a revelation. I am speechless and deeply amazed at this feeling I have never tried before: a deep love, a connection like a thick mass of energy that embraces my soul. I have no idea how to describe this when I return to Denmark, besides just saying that my heart overflows in awe.

I get up again and say goodbye to Baba with this stimulating, bubbling sensation. Then, with my hands gathered in front of my heart, I bow my head respectfully.

"People will forget what you said, people will forget what you did, but people will never forget how you make them feel."
~ Maya Angelou

I AM NOT just walking and smiling. I hover above the large newly washed tiles, now completely visible along the riverbank. The sounds around me are light, bright tones. The high notes only angels can sing—my stomach growls. The scents gathered from all the small kitchens nearby generated my first hunger for several days. I have gone from feeling nothing to feeling every- thing in just a short time. The chuckling smiles from cheerful children playing hide-and-seek behind the fabrics on the clothes- line. The cleansing of the pilgrims in the Ganges River while singing.

The beautiful golden sun still embraces me, but now I notice and happily mingle with the constantly smelling cremations with body parts visibly simmering surrounded by fire and embers. I am so close that the ashes from a cremation swirl around in the air, settling like silver fluff on my cheeks. A man with deep dark brown eyes and dense black hair quickly moves my hand down as I try to wipe it off. Telling me, not to, it means happiness. Everything is beautiful, almost looks staged as in a movie. Fami- lies of the many deceased gather to sing and cleanse in the river, while they push small bowls with flowers of green bamboo leaves neatly braided together. All of what seemed normal and what I otherwise would have distanced myself from. It is as if here, right here and now, no boundaries are being violated. Great respect for the people and their authenticity suddenly makes it very normal to witness. I walk around with ashes on my skin from burning people. It welcomes happiness. I am present, even more than ever before.

While the euphoria is still buzzing, I discover a man following me, or at least I think he is. The figure walks right behind me, and quickly I turn around. My eyes meet a handsome, tall, middle-aged man. His hands rest on the grips while a small monkey sits on the handlebar. The cute little light brown face looks around curiously. Slowly, they follow my steps.

He is not begging like so many others who run around screaming for money. Instead, he is beautiful in his own kind of way. Despite the simple poor exterior, intense energy shows his best side, with tattered clothes and a rusty black bike. He has a sun-bleached olive-green cloth tied around his waist, a bare upper body with a pair of long necklaces, and a scarf around his neck—a cool hippie look. I am fascinated.

The gray-blue black hair is neatly combed, the face is slender and marked with deep furrows, which, together with the gray beard, indicate a mature age. Though smooth skin with firm muscular arms makes me doubt. I continue walking with him right behind me, not afraid, only curious, and I must admit, I kind of enjoy the excitement.

A beginning desire, to study the faces of and souls behind the many people I now notice, reappears. Again, I hear the enjoyable shush sound from winding the film forward. My camera is again being used for its purpose, only to be silent while I change the film, requiring concentration and preferably a break sitting down. The man with the monkey suddenly stops following me, as if an invisible borderline is marked on the street. His face looks at me, but he remains standing while I continue hovering happily.

I look like a typical Scandinavian woman with my long blond thick hair, blue eyes, and 175cm height. I look mature and yet not very aging despite my forty-five years. Laughing out loud and whimsical facial expressions have always come easily to me. Maybe that's where the beginning crow's feet imprinted around my eyes come from. In any case, on the streets of Varanasi, I am just not one of them.

My ambition is to begin a new project here in India, a series of indigenous or tribal people or of persons that just somehow have that "little extra something" face with a story written all over and yet not revealed. I'm exploring authenticity.

The man with the monkey has left a mark on me, an inexplicable track that grows with amazement. Sometimes I experience images or people I can't erase from my retina, and he is undoubtedly one of those moments. My canned Coca-Cola sizzles as the metal trigger clicks. I sit down and study a man being crowned by a single, slightly rusty razor blade. Paralyzed and nervous on his behalf, I fall into spells, completely emptying my head of any thoughts. A liberating feeling with minutes of smooth and slow breaths, rubbing the Coca-Cola can on my wrists soothingly, I just enjoy mine now.

Immersed in coziness and impressions by the street scenes, I pull myself together and walk back along the river, right until the man with the monkey reappears in front of me. Gaping, astonished, my heart beating fast. If this is not a sign, my name is not Grit. Our meeting is much more than a mere coincidence. He looks intensely and directly at me, the same place as when I moved on not long ago. It's more than just a facial expression and much more than I could hope for, like the first portrait of my new series, "Listen." It's like he is reading me. Reads the space of my*self* and *now*. And even though it's a space of deep pain, he does not show any pity or sadness, rather an awareness of a state of mind. His energy transmits solid dignity and self-confidence so convincingly, I inhale this energy as if my life depends on it. I accept this thought open-heartedly as a mentor with a purpose who has been waiting for me to come back. I'm not scared at any point. I smile, knowing I just had a snake in my hands. I will call him Monkeyman, the man with the monkey.

My life has changed forever. My husband and best friend have left me with a future where I was to be walking on eggshells of uncertainty. I copy-paste the energy of dignity, like a mantra painted with such a great revelation, I can only describe as a critical event in my life. Now I, even more, want this man to be my first portrait.

"Excuse me. Do you speak English?" I turn towards a salesman further down the stone staircase. The breeze flutters in my pure white lace shirt, my way too short thigh shorts reveal me as a naive tourist. It is not respectable for a woman to show her legs.

"Can you please ask this man if I can take his portrait tomorrow?" I smile with my hands folded in front of my chest, almost begging.

The meeting is set for tomorrow at twelve.

FROM THE EARLY morning, there is stressful activity everywhere and at the same time it's tranquil, almost spiritual at heart. The sun is heavenly warm. My eyes facing the sky, I inhale deeply, my mouth widens up from cheek to cheek as my thoughts fall back on yesterday.

I place my tripod and get the old, heavy, iron camera mounted and the bellows pulled out. The black cloth to pull over my head leans on my shoulder. The light meter hangs like a necklace, and the plate films are sorted in clear bags with the writing, "used" and "not used." A necessity for me to be very structured, as I seem to forget everything around me when shooting the frames. In that state, I am not very technical. It is a symbiosis of silence between the soul being portrayed, the camera, and myself. A meditative state. A place where I never doubt and let my intuition lead the way.

It's noon, and Monkeyman is still not in sight. Annoyed and sad, it suddenly strikes me that he does not have a watch. Oh, silly me. Somehow, this helps my disappointment dissipate. I start looking for other people to take portraits of, and soon I am on a roll, once again in that spell-like state of mine that I love so much.

People gather around me. The crowd of natives and tourists, holding their mobile phones in the air, taking pictures of my whimsical camera, is getting bigger and bigger.

Oh! If only he would come soon. I sigh. My stomach once again feels the importance of Monkeyman as my very first portrait, which is sent off with a touch of hope I can't let go of.

Time passes and bags for the plate films are opened as needed. The crowd is growing, curiously getting closer as a circle of evidence. Small drops of sweat trickle along the bridge of my nose. It's so hot underneath the black cloth while gently measuring the bellow back and forth, sharpening with a narrow eye in front of the magnifying glass. A sudden intensity twirls my stomach. A slightly airy, cool breeze roams me. Curious, I pull out from under my hot cloth while instinctively turning my head to the left. The crowd slowly opens and paves the way for a path between people. I stare, and my heart gasps. Once again, he stands there, with his combed blue-black hair, hands on the handlebars, and the monkey sitting there. No one would think it has been twenty-four hours since our first meeting with the same green scarf, loosely hanging necklace, and a bare upper body. He is the man I've stood up for today. Knowing how vital my dignity is, this picture will be like a portal for me. Angels sing beautiful tones to my ears.

This mentor gives me strength with just one word in his expression. Even more spectators along the riverbank have gathered up, while I do not yet know how great or significant the condition is being created within me. I only take two frames. Yet, I know everything is just as it should be.

That night, I slept heavily for the first time in many days. I dreamt that my apartment was flooded by clear water up to my knees, but I was not scared.

THE WINDOW IS CHILLY. There is a little condensation at the edge of the oval window, but I do not care and still lean relaxed towards it. The plane is full. We are closely packed in between all the travelers. The light in the cabin is turned off. The air purifier sucks out the last spicy food smell. I tuck the blanket around me, curl my pillow under my chin and pray for some sleep, but peace doesn't come easily as I visualize the children before me and get upset. Suddenly, I remember that my husband and I will pull the rug beneath them away and tear their safety net apart in a few days. It only takes a few seconds to change our family and tear the glossy paper photo into small pieces with all five of us. I am reminded of my dignity, mantra's portal, and commit to myself.

I hereby choose not to be bitter and remain true to myself. After all, my husband and I are getting a divorce, not the children from either of us.

"I dream my painting and then I paint my dream."
~ Van Gogh.

I wonder what the message could be. My duvet is getting way too hot. Yearning, I lift the fluffy edge a bit. The fresh air feels soothing. The luminous sunrays brighten the sheet in front of my pillow gently. I lay my face right there on the sunspot. I smile. I am awakened. And yes. I must remember to write it all down. The encounter with the two very different and wise mentors in India has enriched with gifts of great importance. Now as I flash back to my spiritual awakening, I like wise recall my childhood and all the feelings of the recognizable shadow of loneliness. A search for what I deep down know, and have always known, exists. Paradoxically, I had to take a trip to the other side of the world, far away from Denmark, holding my little prism in my hand, enlarging the words I had chanted again and again. As in a fairytale, they became the small seeds to follow on the path through rough times. My soul has, as a witness, observed and patiently waited for me to become mature enough to leave the nest, embracing the next act to begin.

I am ready to unseal my closet of shadows and cross the threshold at a point of no return. My comfort zone, the no man's land, a gray zone encased by a large shield of fear. Protective of what was left while the universe repeatedly pushed me gently. Like a tsunami, first warning with a minor wave paralyzing me in a state of stress, I did not grasp the importance of, nor did I have any clue I was untrue to myself. I got better, not completely well, but improved to a level of day-by-day living and returned unknowingly to the no man's land where the grey zone slowly grew larger and higher as the wave yet again rose and pulled all the water up to a mighty force. The universe had returned with the devastating shock wave. A very traumatic divorce, the breakup of what I thought was my calling, accompanied my father's illness and death. Even worse, I didn't like who I had become. I met a pain too profound every time I saw myself in the mirror. I had to start over, actively opt out of the grey zone and seek the help I needed. Perceptive that the universe only sends me what I can handle. For once, I took myself seriously. Most importantly, I know I had been living untrue to myself.

Through the past couple of years, I sought authenticity. I traveled the world with my camera, looking for souls who possess what I seek. Mirrored their eyes, listening to the language without words, energy containing all the values, I feel such great importance. In Denmark, I took my time becoming. Meditating in visual self-therapy sessions, silent transcendental meditation, joining spiritual circles, attending breath-work workshops, igniting my creativity as an artist, and mostly, walking along the beach at the north shore for endless hours searching for something I could not label, a definition of myself. Everything I did with kindness, embracing vulnerability, and with a flow of knowing when to act and when to mute and work in silence. Slowly, I am beginning to understand the difference between doing and being.

My body tingles with a rush of energy. Suddenly, it dawns on me that I have lived outside my body in pretty much everything I have executed. The voice from within almost giggles at my self-knowledge. Growling noises abruptly stop the voice. I'm hungry but choose to overhear, curious of more to come. Intuitively, I rise from the comfy sheets, stretch my lazy back, accompanied by a noisy yearn and assume a tailoring position with my hands open, resting on the bare, soft knees. My eyes meet the dignity.

The huge portrait of Monkey man is hanging proudly on the wall in front of my bed. His intense eyes still tell the story. I am ready to receive.

"You are love. You are unique. Look from your heart, not towards your heart. Your inner truth is as simple as what you are and stand for—your love and values. You have done well, danced a marathon with the challenges and shed light on the richness you consist of. The gold that was right beneath you all the time. The eye sees the soul and reconciles."

Proudly I hear myself whispering, "I am—I am love."

"Being me, I live my story."

"Once you awaken you will have no interest in judging those who sleep."

~ James Blanchard

CHAPTER SEVEN

See No Ego, Feel No Ego

By Suzie Curiel

"Nooooo! Nooooo! Nooooo! Javiiiii!!!!!!! Por qué!!!" The blood-curdling screams echoed inside the walls of the small office. My heart pounded a mile a minute. The river of tears had stained my white blouse while the blubbering continued. I took both knees to the floor and covered my face with my hands, shaking in disbelief. I felt like I was drowning and gasping for air. Somehow, I knew it; my gut was hollering at me when my gaze met the pink slip the office clerk held in her hand as she came bouncing into my classroom minutes earlier. When she handed me the note, my stomach churned. My sister-in-law's simple message that read, "Call home immediately," made me feel dizzy. My heart sank! I rushed over to the front office to make the call. I began fumbling the first available phone. The principal caught a glimpse of me and said, "Don't use that phone. Use the one in my office." Once inside, I heard her tell the secretary to close the door behind me. My hands were clammy, and sweat had started to drip down my forehead as I misdialed the number a couple of times before getting it right.

The dial tone buzzed once, twice, then, "Hello?" It was my aunt.

"Hello," I uttered nervously.

"Mija, where are you?" she said.

My voice quivered. "At school—working—why?"

"Don't go anywhere. I'm going to pick you up."

"But, I have my car here... What's going on?" I asked.

"I'll see you in a few minutes," she continued.

"But, why?" I insisted.

"Because Javi died today," she replied. And that was the precise moment when my anguish broke my cool and took the shape of an emotional meltdown.

On the ride home, my thoughts appeared to be moving at the speed of light. One moment, I was thinking about and replaying all the events that had occurred during the last couple of days leading up to the current cruel reality. The next moment, I was thinking about my mom and how the news would crumble her heart and her faith, just like the twin towers crumbled on 9-11.

Once I arrived home, I was limp. I dreaded walking inside. My main concern was discovering my mom's emotional state. After all, it was her eldest son and my brother, our precious blood, that we were mourning on Mother's Day. I made up my mind that Mother's Day would never be happy from that day forward. How does a mother celebrate a holiday that's meant to honor her gift of bringing children into this world, when one of those birthed, beautiful beings was brutally snatched out of physical existence and out of her life?

I opened the black, wrought iron gate. The front door was opened completely, and I noticed a slew of people gathered around outside and inside the house. They were all familiar, yet my depressive state of mind clouded my ability to identify each person correctly. With my head tilted down and my sight on the ground, I avoided looking at anyone directly in the eye as I walked the path from the gate to the steps leading up to the opened front door. As I walked, one person after another greeted me with a hug and an "I'm sorry for your loss." I walked inside and saw a living room full of family looking grim. My dad stood in one corner with a blank look on his face. He has never been a man of many words and he always bottles up his emotions. Then, I spotted my mom sitting on a chair at the dining table.

My cousin was kneeling next to her; my mom's sister stood behind her, gently stroking her short, wavy hair as my mom sobbed with her hands cupping her face. She repeated "why" in Spanish, "¿Por qué? ¿Por qué? ¿Por qué?" My sister and aunt attempted to talk her through her grief, trying to get her to snap out of it for her well-being, telling her she would end up ill if she didn't calm down. That, however, fell on deaf ears. Grief and its stages can be dark and deep, like an abyss. It consumes you quickly and questions your existence.

That afternoon, our immediate family and nieces and nephews piled into several different vehicles and made the trek to Las Vegas, where the tragedy had struck. It was surreal! My mom and I had just returned from Vegas the night before—sans Javi. Our goal was to have him return to Cali with us. He had agreed and then changed his mind. He said he couldn't bear leaving his four kids behind, even though they would remain with their mother, Javi's estranged wife. When my mom asked where he would be staying, he assured her that he would be lodging with his friend until he could find a place of his own.

I couldn't believe that only twenty-four hours had passed, and that would be the last time my mom and I would ever see Javi. It turns out my brother was murdered along with his friend with whom he was supposed to share an apartment. We had tried, to no avail, to convince him to return to California. I went as far as calling the police and requesting their help as though he was a minor, but of course, he was thirty-eight. They probably laughed at the thought when they asked his age.

You might ask, why would we try so desperately to get him to return with us? You see, my brother Javi was a substance abuser. I don't know exactly what substance(s) he was addicted to, but its effects were scary, emotionally draining, and traumatic for all of our family. It was not a good idea to leave him there without a support system since no other family lived there except his wife and his young children. My mom and I had a bad feeling about leaving him behind. That's why, when I saw the pink note while I was teaching, I had a hunch that my fear had manifested. We feared the worst, and the worst came to pass.

The feelings my siblings and I had surrounding his addiction weren't positive. Dealing with an addiction brings about a flurry of negative emotions. At the root of all these awful emotions stand depression, anger and pain. The pain that this God-for-saken entity in the shape of recreational drugs robs an abuser of his sober identity. It destroys the person's ability to make rational decisions and, in turn, destroys entire families in the wake of it.

There were countless times when I was so pissed at Javi. First, I believed my brother was selfish to put my mom through hell by making her worry when she didn't know his whereabouts or that he asked for money and made up excuses as to why he needed it frequently and sometimes in large amounts. Second, I was pissed at him for not being more responsible and making a decision to stay sober for his kids. Third, I was pissed at him for stealing our valuables so that he could get afix. Finally, I was pissed because this was a never-ending story that was causing my mom to be a nervous wreck during the day and lie awake at night, crying silently so that we wouldn't hear her sadness.

And then, when Javi passed, something happened that made me realize I could no longer be mad at him. I could no longer blame him for how others believed he had wronged them or how they thought he had made them feel. It was me I needed to take a closer look at. It took going through this pain of losing my brother to narrow my focus on one of my demons. The culprit here was my ego! I did not realize this soon enough because I was dealing with denial, the first stage of grief.

When guilt set in, I looked for answers. I kept asking myself, "what if…" and "if only…" I had flashbacks of events and conversations spanning several years, leading up to the fateful day my mom and I saw him. What replayed in my mind the most was the last day. In our final moments together, Javi pulled me aside and asked me to give my brothers and sister a message. He said, "Please tell them that I'm sorry for everything I've put you all through. I promise I'm going to get my life back in order. I love you guys." Then, he hugged both of us, and we watched him walk in the opposite direction as we drove off and made our way back to California.

I felt so shitty that my brother's last conversation with me involved an apology, and I didn't get to tell him everything I wanted to say because my ego was standing in the way. I knew my mom was hurting because he had decided to stay, so I thought he deserved tough love. I had told my mom on the way to meet him that she shouldn't give him any money because she would make matters worse by enabling him. She needed to stop giving him handouts unless she wanted to contribute to his continued addiction. My brothers, sister, and I were constantly at war with my mom because we wanted her to be firm with him.

All the while, I didn't realize it was my ego who had taken control regarding Javi and his well-being. As a family unit, I believed that we had collectively given Javi more than enough help, and we should not give any more. I thought he had taken advantage of our generosity and kindness, and enough was enough! However, this could not be further from the truth. The truth is that I allowed my ego to take precedent over compassion. I let my ego overshadow my brother's needs, thinking he didn't straighten up simply because he chose not to.

At the time, my ego didn't allow me to see further than what I wanted to see. It was because I was so focused on what I believed he was doing wrong that I lost sight of the most important thing: love—showing him love. After all, he deserved to be loved. The ego that resided in me wanted him to change and be more like me and the rest of my siblings. However, we all know that we are not in control of changing anybody. Believing that someone will change because we want them to is merely an illusion, and we only end up harming ourselves and creating distance with the other person in the process.

In my quest for answers on self-healing, I concluded that learning to quiet my ego would be the gateway that would lead me to awaken to my inner truth.

First and foremost, what is ego? How do I articulate it? According to Oxford's definition, [Ego is] "a person's sense of self-esteem or self-importance." In a video on ego, Deepak Chopra explains that whenever you feel separate—in other words, "feeling that there's me and then there's the rest of the universe,"—that's the sign that the ego is acting up. The only way to deal with the ego is to recognize it as a contraction or tightness in any given part of the body. In other words, ego is psychological, but it also manifests physically in your body. I also believe that the need to be in control or correct surfaces as side effects of the ego. Once again, these feelings bring about how we feel "separate" or disconnected from others.

What is the driving emotion of the ego? According to Dr. Shefali, "Fear is the emotion that underpins the ego." The ego is the feeling of the "false self." I'm certain that we, as humans, have had feelings of the "false self" as well as the experience of the ego acting out, as Deepak Chopra points out. Deepak Chopra also mentions the simple act of bringing awareness to the ego in the localized part of the body where it constricts, softens it and allows it to dissolve.

My next question was, "How exactly do I overcome my ego in the long run?" Learning to quiet my ego required that I become raw and vulnerable. Becoming vulnerable meant that I had to face something bigger than myself and that I had been putting it off for many months. I didn't even realize that this thing that I didn't want to acknowledge was tearing me apart.

The answer was always in front of me, and it remained there, in the act of forgiveness. There's a stigma around forgiveness that we must address. The act of forgiveness does not mean that what happened between you and someone else is O.K., and now you are pardoning each other. You don't even have to ask another person for forgiveness. To me, this was the toughest part. I had not yet learned that forgiveness does not equal making amends. I was seeking to make amends, which was never going to happen because Javi was no longer with us. I also didn't know then that forgiveness is more powerful than making amends. I always had it ingrained that I needed to hear the words of forgiveness from the other person I felt I had wronged. After my brother's passing, I prayed that wherever his spirit was, he would forgive me for not being there for him like I should have and accusing him of my negative feelings towards him. This emotion dragged on, and it made me bitter.

I learned that forgiveness is never about another person. Forgiveness is a gift you give yourself. As much as we would love to change the past to get a different outcome, we can't. The only hope in gaining your power back lies in your ability to forgive yourself. This holds for both scenarios: whether you wronged someone or felt someone wronged you. Nelson Mandela says, "Forgiveness liberates the soul. It removes fear. That's why it's such a powerful weapon." This goes hand in hand with what Dr. Shefali describes surrounding the emotion that underpins ego: fear. Therefore, when you forgive, you let go of ego.

These are the steps I took for forgiveness:

1. Decide that you want to forgive. No one can do this for you. You have to do it for yourself to be free.
2. Accept that you can only control yourself. Everyone has free will.
3. Write in detail how this situation has made you feel. Only then will you be able to open up entirely and not leave any lingering feelings behind. Be completely honest with yourself.
4. Say it out loud. I forgive (insert name) for (insert wrongdoing). This also includes you forgiving yourself.
5. Remember that forgiveness is a process, and you may have to come back to revisit it. Sometimes, you have to

practice these steps several times before you truly feel the forgiveness come through.

In summary, using forgiveness as a tool will dissolve the emotion of fear, A.K.A. ego.

Grief robs you of your present; it robs you of beautiful moments; and it robs you of your precious time. You never get over it. You only learn to navigate through it by allowing yourself the gift of forgiveness.

To recap, I learned that I can overcome my ego in three simple, yet not always easy, steps.

These are the steps that I took to quiet the ego:

1. Acknowledge that your ego is acting up, and recognize the area in the body where it feels constricted or tight, and keep your awareness there.
2. Use forgiveness as a tool to set you free.
3. Repeat steps one and two whenever necessary.

In my experience, it's important to point out that the ego will be a recurring theme in our lives, simply because we are human and nobody is perfect. However, I learned to pay attention to those moments when they arise. And diffusing them immediately helps to identify those moments faster. Over time, you gain more empathy for yourself and others. You may also start to feel, as I have, more acceptance of others as you come to realize that everyone is doing the best they can with what they have in their current moment.

I also became faster at identifying when others are at a crossroads with their ego. Such was the case when I wrote the following poem. I wrote this poem for a specific person and love interest (M.R.), who will forever hold a special place in my heart. I wrote this poem to communicate in an empathetic way that love has a way of transcending beyond any negative emotion when we are open to receiving it. When I wrote it, it had a very profound significance and it always will.

MARK, MY HEART

I'm speaking to your heart.
Don't let your ego eavesdrop.

I have a message to convey.
I hope your heart will hear this.
I won't have it any other way.

So many times, we hurt.
Whether it be words or actions gone astray.

When the words have left our lips,
or our actions, or lack thereof, manifest
and cause us to feel awkward or in dismay.

I want your heart to hear my message.
Pure and naked, with all the blooms it brings your
way. For there is truth in what I say.

Your ego wants to be right, and almost always, right
away.

Meanwhile, your heart, it knows of true intentions.
It won't steer you the wrong way.

110

When I tell you that I love you,
I hope the words will carry you a long way.

So, I say once more,

I'm speaking to your heart.
Don't let your ego eavesdrop.

I have a message to convey.
I know your heart will open up and listen.
I won't have it any other way!

One day, as I was re-reading it, I had an epiphany. The poem wasn't only about the person for whom it was intended. The poem also spoke to me. The message I received is that I must engage my heart whenever I feel my ego acting up. So, I ask you, reader: will this poem inspire you to listen to your heart whenever you think your ego surfaces?

Works Cited

"9 Inspiring Nelson Mandela Quotes on Forgiveness." *The Borgen Project*, 30 September 2019, https://borgenproject.org/nelson-mandela-quotes-on-forgiveness/. Accessed 25 February 2022.

Oxford Languages. "ego definition." https://www.google.com/search?q=ego+definition&rlz=1CAYGYA_enUS912&oq=eg&aqs=chrome.0.69i59j0i20i263i433i512j69i57j0i20i263i433i512j46i433i512j69i61l3.11511j1j4&sourceid=chrome&ie=UTF-8. Accessed 25 February 2022.

"Removing the Ego." *YouTube*, 25 January 2019, https://www.youtube.com/watch?v=2lK8WNC5V9g. Accessed 25 February 2022.

"What's the Driving Emotion of the Ego?" *Dr. Shefali*, 14 July 2016, https://www.drshefali.com/whats-driving-emotion-ego/. Accessed 25 February 2022.

"The true awakening takes place within."

~ Unknown

CHAPTER EIGHT

Poetry in Motion: A Day in The Life of JeNeil

By JeNeil Miles

I can't turn down, and I've been sitting in the dark for a long time.

Allowing my soul to cultivate my heart and my mind,
so many joked about me being crazy that the laughter
turned into reinforcing the comedy into my identity.
Got me thinking that my thinking needs extra tinkering,
then it turns out that there are many processing like me.
So never again will I accept insanity, especially since I have
found serenity.

Unfortunately, some can't accept that I think differently,
so trapped in familiarity that they're unwilling to see
beyond the surface of their perspective. Instead of being reflec-
tive, they watch others and take corrective considerations when
they really need to buy a mirror and face it.

As a kid, I had a vast imagination, but I didn't have those big, tangible dreams so many others had. You know, like a dream job, a dream house, or a dream car. Instead, I was always lost in a sea of fantasy. I transformed all that

I saw around me into miniature movies, with my action figures being the actors.

I was an avid reader in first grade, although my teacher didn't realize it. Unfortunately, the books she provided me with were not as exciting as the books my mom bought me. By the end of first grade, I couldn't take it anymore.

"Ms. Martin,"I said, my hand raised.

"Yes, Neil?"

"Can I read those books?" I pointed to a section for kids with a higher reading level than me.

She replied enthusiastically, "Of course you can!"

I was stunned. Just like that, I had access to what I had wanted for the entire year. My issue was that I was waiting to be deemed worthy by someone who did not recognize my ability. Speaking up and seizing those books brought me to another level of confidence. I was seven. Let's fast-forward twenty-three years.

As a thirty-year-old, even high school felt like it was ages ago. I was no longer an awkward youth bending to the wishes of the various adults that took turns supervising me. Now I was fully responsible for my actions and decisions. Yes, people still recommend things I should do, but *I'm a grown man, baby! I do things my way!*

And my way is this: just like when I was a kid when my action figures transformed into actors in the movie of my imagination. I like every day like it's my own personal movie and the cameras are constantly rolling. I do not believe in the *same old same old* because I'm expecting something new every day. So, it's only fitting that I attract such a variety of opportunities and circumstances that keep my life suspenseful. I can't settle for a boring life when the world is a playground with so many interesting people willing to allow me to play minor roles within their life movies.

Baby, I'm a star within the galaxy shining like I'm supposed to. Here to shine bright with those who know and help bring revelation to those not yet woke. My mother named me JeNeil Kahree, with the surname Miles, hoping to be different. I'm not sure what that difference looked like in her mind, but her baby boy grew up and evolved into someone amazing.

I would like for you to take a glimpse into my life and see how the universe works with it for the sake of humanity. It is my soul's belief that we are all connected, and despite the many dividing factors, ultimately, we are all one.

February 5th, 2022

It was a Saturday and also one of my off days. Many people my age like to sleep in on their off days, especially if they are accustomed to waking up to begin getting ready for work immediately. I'm a special case.

I don't wake up for work. When my alarm goes off, I'm picking up this sack of flesh and taking it to a gym called Rocking Bootcamp. Where I live, it's common for people to fear getting older around the time they reach twenty-five. I try to embrace every year with the mindset of not letting two digits have so much control of my identity. I'm also fortunate to have a loyal, smart, and encouraging woman in my life whose only flaw is telling me things that I most likely need to hear.

"You're doing Rocking Bootcamp and kickboxing?! You have to find time to rest! I don't think you should work out on the weekends." That's Brelyn, my Butterfly Goddess, so sweet that I hear the songs of newborn hummingbirds every time she speaks.

So as you may have guessed, I wasn't waking up to work out that day. But nevertheless, I was up and moving, getting a jumpstart on enjoying this marvelous day of not clocking in for someone's company.

Maybe the reason I didn't have particular dreams for my life when I was a kid was because I liked so many things and was afraid of being limited to a rigid life of just one thing. The house Brelyn and I rent together is a three-bedroom, with a garage and a back patio. We've turned one room into a creative space, where I usually record music, and another into a treasure room, where we always find cool things we forgot we owned. We have two troublesome cats are running around at all times of the day, and a pitbull mix that enjoys our loving attention and going on any kind of adventure. I don't really know what the American dream is, but my life is good.

When the time turned *7:09*, my "just in case you're still asleep" alarm went off on my phone. Not good. I dashed from the kitchen to our bedroom to silence the alarm, but it was too late.

"Who sets their alarm on the weekend?!" complained Brelyn. She turned over slowly to face me with her eyes half-open.

I had a silly look on my face, as if I was a kid being caught stealing out the cookie jar. "Ahhh...my bad." I turned the alarm off for Sunday. "Good morning!"

Her eyes were still adjusting to the sunlight breaking through the blinds. "Good morning…why are you up already?"

"I got tired of laying down."

"You're crazy," she grumbled. She then did a big morning stretch. "Don't you have a game today?"

"Yep!"

"What time?"

My forehead wrinkled. "Um… twelve… ish. I'll recheck the schedule."

Brelyn yawned deeply. "Okay, boyfriend," she said in a voice I thought was cute. "Are you excited?"

Was I excited? Of course I was! Of my seven seasons of coaching youth basketball, this had been my favorite. I felt more seasoned, organized, and not as stressed in my life. This allowed me the time and energy to provide these boys adequate attention and creativity in planning practice. One of the best compliments I've gotten this season was from a parent, "You must have played school ball!"To his surprise, I told him that I did not!

When I was eight years old, sports weren't even an interest. The first time I played basketball was with my older cousins on a ten-foot goal. I was short and not strong enough to get the ball to the hoop! As discouraging as that was, I didn't completely disassociate from basketball. I loved cartoons and video games. If you know anything about the '90s, basketball icon Michael Jordan made a movie with the Looney Tunes characters called *Space Jam.* Oh, how I loved this movie! That same decade, one of the popular gaming systems was the Super Nintendo. Seeing how much I loved *Space Jam*, my mother bought me the *NBA Hangtime* game. I spent countless hours playing that game and having epic matches against my cousins and friends.

As time went on, video games became more advanced, and I became more athletic. By the time I was a middle schooler, I had played *NBA 2K5* on the PlayStation 2. This game taught me about team chemistry. As you played through virtual basketball seasons, you were allowed to make choices that dictated how well the players on your team got along. Naturally, this affected their performance on the court. My brother, Tanner, and I absorbed what we saw in this game and took it onto the real-life court. When playing together, we won more games than we lost.

I never desired to take basketball to a greater level, but I was fascinated by it. The better I got at it, the more I could use it as a social token. Still, I never imagined myself being a coach!

But in 2013, when my friend Chuck Rose, the athletic coordinator of Foley's Youth Sports at the time, asked me if I was interested in coaching basketball, I wasn't feeling too froggy about it. Basketball is a very technical and complex sport that I didn't think I had the patience to teach. So I don't know what possessed me to volunteer. But it was a chance to play a positive role in children's lives. I've had adults do that for me when I was a kid, so it's fulfilling for me to pass on that good energy.

After a few hours of dilly-dallying and half-assed cleaning, it was about that time to hit the road.

"Babe, we need to get going!" I said as I was cramming my foot into my tied shoe.

"I'm almost done!" she yelled from the bathroom.

I went into our garage and started the car. The passenger side was cluttered with a few items, so I quickly threw everything in the backseat to sort through later. When Brelyn finally came out, I smiled.

"Hey, pretty lady." I opened the door for her. "You want to go catch a game with me?"

No matter how many times I've opened the door for her, she still acts like it's the first time. First, she looked me deep into my eyes. Then, the moment slowed down for me, and I basked in it. Her big, round blue eyes have been dominant in my mind ever since I asked her out at a Christmas Eve party back in 2019. It seems impossible to now think there was a time she wasn't in my life.

Before getting with Brelyn, I had thought that I wasn't meant to be in love. I was nineteen when I first seriously considered marrying a woman. At that time, I was heavily involved with a charismatic-like church. It was a positive step for me to become more attuned to spiritual matters. At church, I learned that prayer wasn't only about sending up wish lists. I was taught that I could hear back from a higher power. In my practice of divine listening, I was sure that I heard God telling me that I should marry this young lady already pregnant with a child. Whether my hearing was valid or not, the two of us gave it a shot. In my mind, it made sense for me to become a stepfather because I had one! When that didn't work out, it was not easy to recover.

I once had this dream of a woman I was romantically involved with back in high school. She was wearing a royal-blue dress and smiling at me. Inspired, I took to social media to reconnect with her. I can't even start to tell you how excited I was when she messaged back with her phone number! Unable to contain my passions, I began laying it down thick that I wanted to be with her. I pursued her on and off for years, thinking that she was *the one*.

Young, dumb, and lonely...

Thinking about you, thinking about you, thinking about you, yea,
Remembering that time when I had you to myself.

The cool was off. The drinks were on, and we were on the dance floor.

The club is looking at us, but I'm in the zone so
It doesn't matter to a gent what they had to think.
I was on a high because you were my date,
Slave to the Rhythm, but your love was trying to make an exchange.

I don't consider myself a playa. I just got gamer ways,
But these games come from a place of caution.
The way I've behaved in love makes me feel so nauseous
When I sit back and reflect,
So may I be direct
With my questions.
When I go to ask
What it is

I ain't trying to sing love songs,
My feelings are so numb,
But you making me feel so warm
And I can't ignore the feeling.
I ain't trying to be a hero,

But you are holding me back from being a villain.

The night at the Christmas Eve party came very close to not happening. The day before had not ended on a good note. Once again, I had found myself disappointed about things not working out with another woman. I considered a new approach to life: make money, play video games, and have a lot of sex with no strings attached.

Before my dive into virtual addiction and sexcapades, my conscience was bothered because I had promised Shannon that I would make it to the party. I thought highly of Shannon and felt bad that I had missed so many other events she invited me to. I planned to hang out for an hour or two and then dip out to go home and play *Skyrim*.

When I showed up at the party, people seemed happy to see me! No matter how shitty I feel, when I am around a group of people I like, I can't help but put on a smile.

When I saw Brelyn, my goal was to be polite and keep it moving. I didn't know much about her, but we had talked once before and I thought she was super attractive. She wanted to speak to me, but I was still somewhat doubtful. Finally, with nothing to lose, I stood next to her and struck up a conversation. I became very intrigued when she mentioned that she was a Special Education teacher.

"I want to teach as long as I can!" She spoke in a way that reminded me too much of a dreamer.

I scoffed at the idea. "Heh, really? Don't you think you're going to burn out before then?" Of course, it was out of my character to be like this, but I was not feeling optimistic.

123

Her eyes hardened, which cut into my soul. "So, you're one of those people?"

Did I fully know what type of person she was talking about? No, but I for sure didn't want to be that guy. Somehow, I managed to get myself out of that potential setback. As the conversation continued, she asked, "What is your passion?"

I wasn't accustomed to women asking me questions like that. It was usually the other way around. "Well…"And it was at that moment I felt that dark cloud lift. "I just really enjoy people. It's something about this world that I find beautiful and terrible at the same time. Every time I decide to quit the world, something draws me back to it. That's probably one of the reasons why I like to write! Whenever I share my writing and see that people can relate, it gives me a sense of hope. It reminds me that we are all in this together. That maybe we'll all wake up and tear down these divides that keep us against one another."

I've been told that I could be too much of a philosopher and that if I wanted to find a woman, I would have to tone it down. Well, I refused to do that because it took a lot of work to get that far in being myself. But, thankfully, Brelyn was drawn to the way I articulated my mind. And there was something about being here with her that allowed me to speak the truth in my heart clearly.

That party became all about her for me. Though I was nervous, I managed well enough to ask her for a kiss while standing under the starry night. As if things weren't mushy enough, I found myself saying, "I don't want to be with anyone else. I would like only to see you…"

Those were the words that sealed the deal!

***

It didn't take us long to get to the gym. Most of my boys were already there and they were hype as usual. When the game before us ended, I rushed my boys onto the court so we could start warming up. This was going to be a tough matchup.

When the referee blew the whistle, I put my starting five on the court. Then, as I focused on the kids, I tuned out everyone else in the gym.

"Alright, y'all! Let's go!"

The other team had this one kid that I thought was the best player in the league. I knew he would be a problem for us, and he confirmed it immediately. As if he was a fly, he weaved through my boys' defense, making his first three shots without seeming to break a sweat.

"Yo, this kid is crushing y'all by himself! We need defense! Deeeeefennnnnse!"

When the kid went to score again, Jaxon put pressure on him and forced a miss. A.J. grabbed the rebound and dribbled to half-court. He saw that Landon was open and made the pass. Landon caught the ball, dribbled to the front of the rim and shot.

SCORE!

This brought my team back to life. Kaycen and Cash began locking down Kid Awesome from the other team, which encouraged him to pass more. Fortunately for us, he was the strongest shooter on the team, so this disrupted the flow of their game a bit.

When I subbed in my biggest and tallest player, Liam, I was excited to see him moving with purpose. A few weeks back, he had admitted that he was playing basketball to lose weight; but today, he looked like he was there to win.

Once I got Baylor and Stephen in the game, it made me proud to see them playing with more energy than usual. Again, basketball is a highly complex sport that not every kid picks up. Though they were a bit slow on some things, they gave the other team hell!

As the game progressed, I watched A.J. make a shot as he was knocked to the floor. Once the ball went through the net, the crowd went nuts!

"Yes!"

My team made another defensive stop, and this time, Jaxon passed Cash the ball. Being one of the faster kids on our team, Cash jetted down to the goal and made a quick shot. It was his first goal of the season, and I was hype!

Kaycen made it his personal goal to play defense on Kid Awesome. Though he would score every so often, Kaycen was not allowing him a leisurely walk through the park. The solid defense allowed Jaxon to score multiple fast-break baskets that kept us in the game.

Despite the fantastic game my kids played, we lost by two in the end. Yet, I couldn't be more proud of those boys for how they played like a team.

"Bring it in!" As each kid approached me, we slapped hands. "Chin up! Y'all played like warriors out there!"

I came into this season with the intent of not being overly concerned with winning. Don't get me wrong, I love to win; but there were other kinds of victories I had my sights on. My goal was to ensure that the boys were having fun, that they would learn more about basketball, and that their confidence would be built up week by week and game by game. So every chance I could, I was instructing, encouraging, or pushing them to grow. I wanted them to move as one and not just focus on individual success.

My position in these kids' lives is very interesting, because I know that they are being confronted by a multitude of beliefs. I don't state this to the parents plainly, but I try to deliver certain truths within the instruction I present to them. Truths like speaking good upon your existence; the power of manifestation; and using intuition to be engaged with your surroundings.

I am convinced that they are undergoing things that they may not be able to understand or clearly speak on yet. From the lessons learned from my own battles within, I hope to leave these kids with shards of lights to help them on their life journey.

After the game was over, the rest of the world came back into focus. Though I wasn't the one playing, I felt drained. My lady stood patiently in front of me, waiting for me to acknowledge her presence. It took me a moment to withdraw from my head, but her smile warmed me once I did.

"Good job, Coach!"

I wrapped my arm around her shoulders. "I love you." And then I kissed her forehead.

Later that night, we made the drive out to Pensacola, Florida, to attend the Imbolc party hosted by our friends Charlie and Sam. Charlie explained that Imbolc is all about the midpoint transition from winter to spring. It is a holiday about letting go of the old and transforming into the new.

I met Charlie back in 2013 through my friend Alex. While we were working at a grocery store, Alex heard me freestyle rapping and kept insisting that I go to Charlie's studio. Finally, though I didn't feel ready, I caved.

When I got there, I was super nervous, but I wanted to look like I knew what I was doing. Before even talking about music, Charlie wanted to feel who I was. He took me on a drive through his studio's small town and even introduced me to some of his family.

During our short trip, we talked about religion, spirituality and synchronicities. Despite coming from entirely different backgrounds, we had similar outlooks. This made it easy for me to be transparent about my inexperience in recording music.

He was chilled about it and encouraged me to go into the booth and freestyle a few times over the beat he made. It didn't take me long to come up with words, especially with the instrumental jamming like it was. Together, this is what we made:

Another man got shot today
But I think we can find a way.
Let love be the remedy,
Breathe life into humanity.
Words are power, G.
Speak and make-believe
(Yes)Speak and make-believe

Speak and make-believe!

That day was the beginning of brotherhood.

When Brelyn and I made it to the house, I could hear music playing inside. But, when I knocked on the door, the music stopped.

"Who is it?!" I heard someone yell.

"Balance!" Which is a nickname of mine.

The door swung open to reveal Dalton's smiling face. He hugged us and practically dragged us into the house. Charlie was sitting holding his guitar with Kaitlyn next to him. Dalton went and sat back down in a chair next to Kaitlyn, and beside him was Corey. Next to Corey was Kris, and sitting in a random beach chair was Sam. Next to her was Allison and then Grant. Finally, Alex was sitting on a cajon drum.

We hugged everyone in the room. Charlie placed the guitar down and grabbed a Ziplock bag holding leaves.

"We saved some for you," he said with a smile. "We already have the fire going. You remember what we're doing, right?"

"Yea, I'm sacrificing the sweaters Brelyn likes to dress our dog in," I said with a sly grin on my face.

Brelyn punched me in the shoulder. "I'll sacrifice you."

We both took a leaf, and Allison gave us markers. I took a few steps away from everyone to write down what I wanted to sacrifice to gain more focus for my creative endeavors. Once I was done, I walked over to the fire and tossed my leaf in. When I found an empty seat to sit in, I saw that I managed to miss the flame!

I pointed it out to everyone, "It said, you can't sacrifice me, I'll sacrifice you!"

Dalton bravely stuck his hand in and pushed the leaf further into the flames. "There you go, buddy!"

I sighed in relief. "And this is why I need a support group!"

Charlie sat back down on the couch with his guitar. Alex drummed his hands on the cajon as Charlie strum chords from familiar songs. The room was singing words to pieces made by GreenDay, Prince, and Metallica. Eventually, the two got tired, and Alex got up from the cajon.

Charlie looked at me and asked, "Bro, you want to kick a free-style?"

My eyes lit up. "Fo' sho!"

Everyone in the room knew I rapped, but not all had seen my freestyle. I was surprised how quickly they became quiet in anticipation of hearing me. Charlie strummed his guitar, creating a chilled tune. I took a moment to feel the music and looked around the room for a starting point. My eyes gravitated to the coffee table:

Looking at this table
I am able
To retrieve words from deep within,
No need for paper or the pen,
Especially when I can project words from the center of my head.

I got the vision of a man locked in,
Like a madman in a straight jacket
I'm blackin'
out; erasing any doubts placed within my mind
Back in time when I wasn't quite aligned
With the purpose I've been given from a divine place,
These dollars I no longer chase,
I'd rather place myself in peace,
Allowing good energy to guide me
To a place of deep; beyond carnal understanding.
Not worried about a brand name; I let my actions represent me
I live to be free, and I refuse to be
Another prop for false reality
Being displayed on the T.V. screen,
I'd rather you see me. . .
B-A-
L-A-
N-C-E
I spell it out in hopes of you catching the magic.
Some do this for the clout. I do it for the passion,
I bend rhymes like I was made of elastic,
I'm like Star Fox meeting the fantastic one,
Taking anything tragic and turning it into positive lessons.
My load had lessened when I determined I'm more than a stone
for stepping
On; I'm a king that has grown from a kid trapped in spiritual
poverty,
Follow me, oh ye that is drained of energy
'Cause you were fooled into giving up your sense of humanity
By being programmed to be another cog in the machine.
I got the Method-man, assembling like Wu-tang
I came to do my thang, no matter the peering eyes.
Some may think I'm insane, but they don't have wings to fly.
So what's a chicken to a hummingbird?

You aren't trying to see the world, just stuck in your limited view
Yet I'm the crazy one, but you're going coo coo,
Oh, how I bless you; may I ruffle your feathers,
I'm here to bring change like the weather,
Rain, sleet, or snow, not enough to stop this parade.
It's Balance Universal, and I will reign for eternity!

When I ended my rhymes, I looked up to see my friends looking at me as if I had just breathed fire from my mouth.

"Bro!" said Corey. "That was badass!"

"I didn't know you could rap that long," admitted Kris.

I looked over at Charlie, and he smiled at me. I could have gone longer, but I wanted to respect the room and not make it all about me. In retrospect, I should have rapped until the walls started to sweat.

After my five seconds of fame, the vibe shifted as we broke out the board games. As the night continued, beer was consumed and laughter was constant. There would come the point where sidebar conversations took over, and the games were forgotten.

Somehow, I found myself sitting next to the fireplace where all our sacrifices were now ashes. I was tired, but I didn't want the night to end. Instead, I found joy in seeing a room of such colorful people engaged in thoughtful conversations and laughter. This was exactly what I wanted in life.

It's times like this when life feels so complete that if death came suddenly, at least it would come during an elated state. Unfortunately, American culture seems to keep us on this treadmill of always reaching for more: money, accolades, and respect. I believe that at some point you have to realize that the most important thing one can possess is *self.*

It's a universe within us, filled with all sorts of treasure.

We need to cherish that.

"Like the lotus flower, we too have the ability to rise from the mud, bloom out of the darkness and radiate our beauty into the world."

~ Unknown

CHAPTER NINE

Define Your Own Path

By Ivan Budiani

Everyone has a unique journey in life. We all start in different places and we all end up in different places as well. Some of us reach our goals; we find our destination. Others struggle even to find where the path begins. Some paths seem easy. Some paths seem impossible. But we all have our own way, and it is our job to make the most of it. Besides all the typical ups and downs of a girl's life—friends, puberty, marriage, education—there is another uphill battle and many people never reach the top. This is the steep, difficult path to self-discovery.

My path, like yours, has had smooth, easy days and days where the road was muddy and I just wanted to stop walking. But I've kept going, and I hope you do too. I keep putting one foot ahead of the other because my goal, my destination, is self-awareness. And even when it seems far, it is a goal I have chosen and will always work toward.

It's difficult to pick the single day of when a personal journey began. Our thoughts always grow from seeds to plants before becoming actions. But if I had to choose a time when I truly began to take this path seriously, it would have been when I was a teenager. That was when I planted the seeds, when I was wondering what kind of woman I wanted to be. What do I want to achieve? What are my life goals? Where do I see myself in ten years?

***

When I was a little girl, I thought my life would be easy. Everybody would love me. I would be rich and find my Prince Charming as he puts the shoe on my foot. We would have two or three kids and live happily ever after. That was all in my head. As I grew older, I started to find out that there was another path in our lives, one that's not always smooth. Still, we all have to travel that path to reach our destinations, so that's what I did. I stepped my foot into that muddy, cranky path that brought me to this place where I am now. That path led me to something beautiful. It brought me on my self-discovery journey and taught me the self-acceptance I'd always dreamed of.

I remember being a young teen and thinking I would never accept myself fully. I hated myself for being me. When I was a kid, I saw all the other girls my age having perfect skin and playing like normal kids. And there I was, sitting in my room, crying and blaming myself for being sick. I was very sick through much of my childhood, my body covered with painful sores. The hurt was such that I could not even walk properly. This is not an easy thing for me to reveal. I never told anyone about this before as I always wanted others to believe I had the most carefree, perfect life.

Even now, sometimes I don't want anyone to know where I've been, that I've been struggled, that I was an ugly duckling.

My relationship with my inner self also wasn't that good. I never felt enough. I was trying to fix myself as if something was broken inside me. I was so busy looking for acceptance from others, trying to get their approval to feel that I was enough. Then one day, I realized that I was just a people pleaser. I cared too much about other people's opinions about me. I was afraid of being left behind by my friends and society, so I craved constant attention from others. As a result, my life was full of insecurities, self-doubt, and the fear of missing out.

Throughout my school years, I was a straight-A student. My parents' were so proud of me. I also joined several clubs and extra-curricular activities. I was one of the best chess players in my school. All I did was study. I never involved myself with students who didn't have the same vision. I surrounded myself with only friends who had qualifications, friends who got good grades and were never in trouble at school. Focusing on becoming the kind of daughter my parents could talk about in the neighbor-hood was my priority. Back then, I marked it as one of my main achievements.

Don't get me wrong, my relationship with my parents was good. They never forced me to do things. It was just me. I just love the feeling of being a proud daughter. They supported me as much as they could, even spoiled me a little.

My dad was also a chess player. He taught me to play since my early age. He was always excited to hear that I went to some competitions. He trained me so well. He even made a handmade chess board especially for me. My heart was full. Knowing how happy and proud he was made me wants to keep doing my best.

When I was in university, I kept doing the same. I studied hard to maintain good grades for the sake of keeping my scholarship. It wasn't because my parents couldn't pay the tuition fee; I just liked how I felt when I heard them talking about me with the neighbors, telling other people I was smart enough to get that scholarship. This approval was everything to me. No matter how hard I was on myself, I believed that I was okay as long as I got that approval.

I also got myself a boyfriend when I was in university. I found the perfect boyfriend based on the qualifications that I always kept. He was a smart, intelligent, fresh graduate. He was a teacher. He was the type of person who always did things seriously. I thought we were a perfect match. He even helped me with my studies. The relationship went well until the day I found out that he was just too much for me. He started to take control of everything. Don't do this, don't wear that, don't go there, don't, don't. I began to doubt myself. If he had to give me so many rules, maybe I was not good enough. My subconscious mind started to believe that something was wrong with me, and that it was making him unhappy. I did not get his approval that I was a good partner. I began to question my quality.

We finally ended our relationship after three years together. It was not easy for either of us. But I really could not take it anymore. It was too much. It felt like I was sacrificing my mental health to be with him. I guess it because both of us have dominant personalities. So we both demand control over each other. And I thought that was not a good sign for us to stay together. So after a lot of endless conflict and tension, we gave up.

I was broken after our separation. Since then, it's been hard for me to build a serious relationship with a man. My previous relationship caused a kind of trauma deep inside me. I didn't want to be controlled anymore, to be blamed for wearing my favorite outfit, to be reprimanded for basically being me.

But at the same time, I learned a lot from that separation. I learned it was up to me whether I let people control me or not. I always have that choice, to stay or to let go. Choosing to stay meant remaining controlled, unable to became the person I wanted to be. Choosing to let go meant not having him in my life anymore.

I chose the second option. I let him go. I did feel lonely at first, but as time passed, I got my freedom back. This is what I wanted, and it feels good.

Why does it feel good? How can letting go be so positive? That question kept popping up in my head. It feels good because that's my truth, and it's the truth of every human being on the planet. We want freedom of choice.

I kept letting go. People, things, feeling, expectations. This feeling of freedom awakened something inside me. The little me. Someone I wasn't aware of was waiting for me to give her more attention. Unfortunately, I was still too busy focusing on outside things and forgot to give her what she needed. I feel sorry now for being so hard on myself and sacrificing my happiness just to get the outside approval I was always craving. Sometimes I felt her crying silently, telling me she was tired. But as my ambition grew, I ignored her more and more. I kept doing what I was doing until I realized that she was right and that it was time to treat her better and value her effort and sacrifices.

I tell myself that it's never too late to start showing yourself that you are loved. This is where I begin my journey to self-love, self-acceptance, self-awareness, and self-discovery. It has awoken me to who I am now.

One day, I was sitting in an outdoor yoga studio and daydreaming about the past few years as I waited for my yoga class to begin. I had signed up myself for a 200-hour yoga teacher training course. At first, I thought I would take the training so I wouldn't have to hire a yoga teacher for my daily practice once I graduated. But day by day, and training by training, I found something else. I started to think and act differently. It felt like my outer self was more connected with the inner me. It felt like I had found the reason I was looking for in my life—the reason why I was here, the reason why I did things, why I'd chosen to be the person I am now. It was such an eye-opening and game-changing experience. My mindset began to change completely. I didn't see things the same way anymore. It is easier for me to be grateful for every little things in life as previously I was a type of person who really hard to satisfy. I complained all the times and blamed myself a lot. But now, all I could think was, "Wow. This is insane. How can I feel this way?"

Have you ever wished you'd started something when you were younger? That's what I felt at that time. But then I realized, I'm here now. I can start now. I should be grateful for this, for starting the self-discovery journey. So many people out there haven't started yet, but at least I know that I need to.

Some people might say, "You are too young to feel that way. You should really just enjoy your life as young people do." But you know what? They will say the same thing to an older me. So I imagine lying on my death bed, when someone finally says something new. But now they say, "Well, it's too late, darling."

My advice here is, this is your journey. You are never too young or too old to start to feel awakened. It's never too early or too late. Everybody has their own timing. Maybe this is not theirs. Perhaps this time is yours. So do it. Do what makes you happy, for yourself. Take charge of your own happiness. Let go the things that don't serve your values. Don't let the outer argument be your downfall. Don't let people doubt you. Be your own person. Don't let their mantra control you. Find your own mantra and walk your own path. You are on the right track. You are on time.

***

As time flew by, I realized that self-awareness is not always about letting things go. Sometimes it is like finding a present made just for you and having the courage to accept it. One wonderful thing that I have learned about myself is that I love yoga. I love when I know that I can take complete control of my body, my breath, and my mind, following my intuition. I love to feel myself flowing from one pose to the next. Sometimes people say my flow is too active and I should hold the pose longer. Well, I just listen to my body. It tells me to move, so I do.

Yoga has taught me to listen to my body and understand what it needs. When I was younger, I could not stop blaming my body for how it was. When I was sick, I blamed it for being too weak. I didn't understand that it was just trying to tell me to take some breaks and get some good rest. When my skin would break out, I blamed it for being too sensitive. It was just telling me to eat healthier. See? I'm getting better here. I need to be more understanding and be a good listener to my own body.

Yoga is a game changer for me. The more I do it, the more it increases my self-awareness and awakens my self-love. It helped me so much to learn that the love that I was craving from someone else, I could get from myself. I'd never felt this way before. My spirituality became so strong and I was emotionally stable. I started to be able to control how I wanted to feel. Along with this journey, I started to learn to live more simply. I started the vegetarian lifestyle, which I never thought I would do. Changing my eating habits was not that easy at first. I was a big fan of fast food. But since I knew that I needed to take better care of my body, I tried my best to have less of it. Well, I just take it step by step. Slowly but surely, I'll get there.

Also, believe it or not, I do talk with myself a lot. I discuss anything that I want to do with the inner me. I tell her my secrets. Building inward personal trust is an essential thing. As a result, we develop deeper connections and trustworthiness, which helps to bring our self-confidence out.

Perhaps you have heard this phrase: "Of course, I talk to myself; sometimes I need expert advice." Well, that is absolutely true. No one can understand you better than you. So start to talk to them, and make sure to listen to their advice. Give them the time and space to tell you what they needs. Sometimes by taking a deeper breath and giving her enough time to think and talk with you, you will realize what you really need. So from now on, I encourage you to take that deep breath whenever you feel you have lost your direction. Maybe you will need two or three long breaths. That is okay too. Just focus, no matter how long it takes. It really helps.

* * *

Besides doing yoga and being a good listener for myself, there is one more thing that helped me find my path. I started to surround myself with positive and like-minded people. Since I started practicing yoga, I have made more friends from the yoga community. I spend more time watching yoga videos and using my social media only to follow positive people. It is said that you attract what you desire. The law of attraction is real. When you want something, the universe will conspire to help you achieve it.

My circle of friends has changed drastically. I no longer hold onto people who don't match my energy. It is easier for me to let go of a relationship or friendship that doesn't match my values. Previously, I was always so afraid to lose a friendship. I would let them mock me in the name of human connection. I let them call me weird names and laugh at my failures. I was afraid to be left behind. Without noticing it, I let them make me miserable. I had so many "friends," but I wasn't happy.

Since I started this journey, I have met many people who have the same vision as me. They encourage me to be a better version of myself as they are doing the same thing for themselves. In my new friend circle, we learn and grow together. We support one another.

In addition to people, I'm also becoming more mindful of the things that go inside me. I am more aware of what energy I allow myself to absorb. I have started to eat healthier. I know that I have to take better care of my body. It is not a disposable vessel that I can change out when broken. It is a lifetime asset. I've also become more mindful of what goes into my mind. I decided to fill it with more positive affirmations, so I read a lot of self-help and self-development books. Every morning when I wake up, I tell myself that I'm going to have a great day and the universe is helping me to achieve my goals.

***

There are some questions that I used to ask myself along this self-discovery journey, and these questions have become my life template.

The first question is: who do I want to be? I need to know the answer to this question to know where to start and which path I have to choose. Do I want to be a mom? Then I should take the path that leads me to meet my future husband. Do I want to be an independent career focused woman? Then the approach should be one where I can find my dream job and focus my energy there. Or do I want to be a homeless, miserable woman? Then maybe I don't have to bother choosing any path. I can just stay still, doing nothing, lying in my bed all day daydreaming of that Prince Charming. What will you choose? You can decide what you want to be, so take the chance!

The second question is: why do you want that? To achieve your goals, to manifest your dream, you need to have a strong reason. You need to find your why. My why is because I want to be my true self. I want to be who I want to be. Don't get me wrong, I'm happy to be my parents' pride and joy. But I want to do it in my own way. I want them to be proud of me because I am me.

The third and final question is: how can I achieve that? After knowing who you want to be, where, and why, this is where the realization part begins. You need to know the *how*. This is where your vision becomes visible. You can't just have goals without a plan. That's not a goal. It's a dream. A forever dream if you are not going to put in your effort to manifest it. In my case, my how is following my intuition, doing what I love, and freeing myself from controlling behavior. I surround myself with only positive people and do as many positive things to my body. If you want to achieve your goal, you should know your how and implement that in your journey.

***

My journey brought me here. The path is still long, I know. But I'm happy that I have come this far, and at least I know that I have chosen the right path. There are still stones and muddy trails on the way, but since I have passed some of them, I've started to get used to it and know where to step my feet. It is still not easy, but I know it gets easier as I move forward.

This journey has taught me so much. It made me realize the importance of moving forward. If I'd chosen to stay in my comfort zone because I didn't know which path to take, I wouldn't be here right now. If I did not start then, maybe now I would still be there, telling myself that I should have started earlier and blaming myself for not having started yet.

But here I am now, grateful for what I have chosen, what I have been through, and for being who I am now: the girl in my dream. The girl who knows what she wants, what she needs, and what she deserves.

Once again, self-discovery is not just about getting all you want in life. It is also about understanding your loss and why you have to lose sometimes. It doesn't just come from you, but also from the people around you. I will not say that I have discovered everything or arrived at my destination. No. I have a long way to go. But at least I have found my path, which is a good start.

So as I started mine, you should start yours, too. Start to be more intentional with what you are doing and who and what you surround yourself with—knowing your worth. Start to focus on yourself, develop and improve yourself. Build a deeper connection with the inner you. And last but not least, take charge of your happiness. You have complete control of yourself. Be true to you!

"Awakening is not to know what this reality is. Awakening is to know what reality is not. It is to cease identifying oneself with any object of knowledge whatsoever."

~ Alan Watts

CHAPTER TEN

Awakening to My Inner Purpose

By Hugh Dinning

Dear reader,

Twenty-two years ago, I stood alone amongst my family, best friends, and our dog. On a day I wished I could cancel—my 50th birthday.

How could I speak, I had nothing to celebrate. I felt lonely, ashamed, sad, and unworthy. My addiction had dragged me away from forming any real-life relationships. Even my kids. There was always the divider interfering.

So much covering up. Lies, deceit, life had no meaning anymore. I had no one to turn to. My nervous system was at its breaking point.

Five months later, a lump on my neck. What is it? The doctor checks the X-ray. We need more tests. You have a squamous cell mass on your throat. You will need radiation.

My wife is in shock, but I am at peace. What is going on? Lying in bed, a peace flooding my entire body. A soft voice "You have to take responsibility for your own life." The kitten, now a lion. No one can tell me what to do.

Life now had meaning. It was up to me. 22 years later, each day is a celebration. Each night, my head resting on the sweet pillow, you did well, young man. Finally, I am ready to share the journey of my awaking to my true inner purpose with the world.

The journey to the racetrack.

From a very early age, I would be woken up by the sounds "Click clop, click clop". What is this unfamiliar sound? Now awake, in darkness, I crawl to the window. Below a tiny man aboard a prancing horse in our street. So early, so strange to me. Doesn't everyone sleep until sunrise? The next day the same. And again, and again.

Now seven years old, curiosity leads me into a new world. Why are these horses returning to their homes so early in the morning? And every day, it doesn't seem fair. I thought dogs and cats were the only pets that had a home. I must get to know these animals.

On a Saturday, a mumbling sound was finding its way into my head from a far distance place. Every thirty minutes for about two minutes, someone was trying to speak to me. Then it was gone. How strange. Every three weeks, this sound of a voice so keen to talk to me.

I must find it. I found the courage to look for the man teasing me every three weeks. My friend over for the day, we wander together down to the bottom of our street, so many cars. A vast building, with people roaring, it must be a festival. The sound is so clear. He is not talking to me but the people inside. We waited until the speaker spoke no more.

People leaving, some happy, others sad, many angry. This man must be famous. So many go to see him. Why does he make people unhappy?

On the walk back home, the horses who live in my street pass me by. The gates open and home they are. What a strange day, my first visit to the racetrack.

One day, in 1956, my father came home one evening from his day at the office, with a big present for the family. What is this strange brown wooden box with glass cut into the front? Then he puts a plug in the wall, and we see people behind the glass. Wow, dad, where did you find this? TV had hit Australia.

What a gift it was for the wide-eyed boy. Homework was an obstacle to overcome, to reach the TV.

Saturday was my favorite day. No school, early morning sports, afternoon sitting in front of the TV, focused like a formula one driver. Amongst constant updates on the AFL football matches were the horse racing results. It wasn't long before I gathered my favorite jockeys, horses, and trainers. There were horses and a trainer who lived opposite our house. I felt at home with them.

I noticed the newspapers my father brought home had many articles about the upcoming race meetings and who was likely to be the winner. This was when I started to get involved. The highest student indeed could not focus as intensely as I did in sorting out the winners.

Saturday had everything. Playing and watching TV was the new world order for me. I was a very competitive and accomplished sportsman, especially being so small. I was lauded like a prince because of my achievements.

I moved to the senior school which was on a different campus in 1962 at the age of 13. Something strange was going on. Three times as many students and the size of the senior students was overwhelming. And there was a seriousness that was disturbing me. They were so focused on the classroom. I dreaded going to school and facing tests that held no interest for me. I was becoming a nobody.

Worst of all, my teammates were growing overnight it seemed. At the age of fifteen, they had become beanstalks towering over the tiny boy. No longer the star. My ego had taken a dive. I had lost my identity. I loved competing and thought this was life. I had dreams of being an international cricket player for Australia. The dream shattered overnight. Winning was a memory, stripped of what I thought would last forever. My body had let me down. Friends had noticed my depression. I was nicknamed "Moody Dinning".

There had to be another way. My mind frantically searched for the solution. I was stuck at school. I had to fill the empty space with something special. Immediately the racetrack came to mind. I loved the challenge of picking the winner. My heart was pumping again to this tune. This was the inspiration that would be my saving grace. I could be the school bookmaker.

In springtime, there is a big racing carnival in the city of Melbourne. One of the most famous horse races in the world is the Melbourne Cup. The carnival lasts for about six weeks. Most people in Melbourne try their luck in picking the winners of the big races. I took on the role of the school bookmaker. I would offer a punter (a person who wants to bet on the horse they thought would win the race). Each horse would be rated by a bookmaker on its ability to win the race. The word got around the school what I was doing. I had six of the best weeks of my life at school. And I was making some money.

However, six weeks was not enough. I was hungry for more. The racetrack that I had discovered ten years ago, had been waiting for me.

In October 1966, I entered the arena. Little did I know, I was entering a prison that would slowly try to destroy me.

THE ARENA

I felt like a king entering a party celebrating my birthday. Such an excited buzz filled the place. This is life. Not judged, just one big family celebrating my birthday. The occasional frown. "How did they let you in? You are so tiny?" Water off a duck's back. No one could take away my joy. The day was the thrill of my life. A day must end. How to continue was the big question?

Still at school, the classroom was a total distraction. The teacher's voice drifts into one ear and out the other.

Morning tea and lunch break were my panaceas. A small group of like-minded gamblers met during each break. Reviewing the weekends racing and sports. Time went so quickly it wasn't fair.

A question was hovering over me, and the answer was a huge challenge. My pocket money could not serve my needs. My father carried many pound notes in his wallet once a week. Surely not. The tempter was too strong for the little boy. Like a man on a tight rope, I tiptoed into my father's bedroom. Slotting a few pounds into my pajamas, I returned to bed. Sleep escaped me on these evenings.

In my last year at school, something surfaced that eased my pain. My father was also mixing with people in high positions in the horse racing industry. One of his best friends owned many race-horses. And they were trained by the most successful horse trainer in Australia. In 1967, the winner of the second biggest horse race in Australia, the Caulfield Cup, was owned by my father's friend. On the evening of this race meeting, the Caufield cup, the jockey, trainer, and my father's friend celebrated in our home. Later, I discovered my father was a gambler. I had grown up in fertile soil to become a gambler.

At last, life at school had finished. What now? I had wasted my father's money, but not my brothers—top marks for them. Failure and shame, flooding my body.

My loving father found me a job selling clothing in one of the first menswear boutiques in Melbourne. I loved it. The intellect was not needed because worldly knowledge held no interest for me. However, clothing fascinated me, and the manager was intriguing. Unlike my schoolmates from the upper class, he was the first of many Italians I would meet on my journey. He came from very humble beginnings. His father was a grocer. Business, following my father, a new world was opening up, which has lasted the test of time.

I had my own money now, so stealing fell away. What a relief. "I hope God does not exist, or I am in trouble," Were the words humming around me.

I loved working in the shop and became a manager soon after. I started to play with fire. I would borrow money from the till to use for betting. Once weekly, I would do the banking, and somehow it all worked out. The nervous system was screaming STOP. With deaf ears, I marched on within the arena.

A friend of mine and I came up with a business idea selling men's swimming trunks in the model of boxer shorts. My father, who was firmly established in the textile industry, knew a company to manufacture them for us. We had arranged an appointment with the manufacturer to meet and discuss what we needed to prepare so the production could take place. On that evening, a prominent harness racing event took place in the Victorian countryside. I had a choice. Even now, I cannot comprehend how I chose harness racing. The following day, my father knocked on my bedroom door and entered. I was asleep. There was so much he wanted to say, but not a word came from his lips. A sad father then went off to work. I buried my head under the sheets. I was going nowhere. That was the end of my first business. It took a heavy toll on us both.

A few years later, just after my 21st birthday, I took off to the UK. I had to get out of here. The young boy walked up the plank of this rescue ship, the past behind him. No one knew my history. I can start afresh, with new clothes, the masks now in the trash can.

On the balcony, I waved goodbye to my family and friends, not only to them but to the internal rubbish I had left at the bottom of the plank.

My first two tests were Bingo and the Melbourne Cup horse race. My impulses were still alive to the thrill of the chance to be a winner—six weeks of Bingo every night.

Arriving in the UK, I was quickly drawn into the magic of the betting shop. The UK provided me with many more options to try my skill of picking the winner than Australia. I was right, they don't know me, and they don't know what I am doing at home. This freedom tastes like honey. Amongst the glamour of Carnaby street, I was in heaven.

I returned home two years later. Within the first week, I had hit the racetrack with even more passion.

I soon moved out of home and founded a new group of fellow gamblers. Life was a party. Sex, rock and roll, alcohol, and gambling—what a brew. I don't recommend it.

The love of my life had arrived. The tables had been turned. She was the focus. How was this going to work? Naively, I mixed the two because I loved them both so much. I couldn't live without them. The playing field had expanded. The stock market, poker, and the roulette wheel the additions. So active, putting out so many fires, ducking, and weaving, how could I keep up the pace? Love and tension are poles apart. Tired and restless, my body was warning me.

A son was born against my will. I was not ready; I couldn't cope with all of this. The cracks widen. The inevitable happened. The day had come, the shipwreck finally sunk. Everything fell apart; my marriage was destroyed. A pain in my heart lasted for two years. Gambling was no longer exciting, just filling a gap.

My life took a turn in the right direction. I had discovered a will inside of me that was fighting against my addiction. This led me to a spiritual awakening in India. A guru entered my life, and things were changing for the good. But strangely, gambling was still a very active mode of expression.

I began a new relationship, and at the same time was creating a new business. In the high-flying eighties, it took off like a rocket. Money was coming in from everywhere. Oh, how the monster inside of me loved the gift of cash to feed itself. The effort to keep this all together was dragging me down.

My body, my dearest friend, I had left it alone until one day it had had enough: the rash decisions, the love of foolishly handing over my rewards to the greedy bookmakers. Then, the body collapsed, lying unconscious in my office, the business soon followed. My health, self-esteem, and company had been ripped from me by a foe.

My will remained strong, and I had a loving doctor who saved me. I was gifted with a marriage, a son, and a new job. My wife strangely encouraged my gambling because I was often very successful. The tempter was still leading the way.

I started a new business joining forces with a close friend. He taught me the importance of slowing down. Running a business in that way calmed my nerves. On the other hand, he was also a gambler. Stock exchange and horses. I realized some people could be calm and measured about it, but not me. I was a fanatic.

My life split in two. The will, still involved, I was searching for a spiritual pathway that would correct all my weaknesses and the urge not to gamble was the priority. Something had to change. My business partner remained a test. He was a quiet achiever. I was curious how his investments were going. His successes challenged my winning instincts. And jealously was a curse living within me from childhood. His success with stocks and shares, and his winning streaks with the horses, fueled the fire to beat him. I surely could do better than him. The betting was less frequent, but the size of the bet was a lot larger. This was getting me into trouble. The amounts lost were scary.

My diagnosis strengthened me. I was taking responsibility for my own life. I cleaned out the closet. Sadly, a dysfunctional marriage was a casualty. The spiritual journey held no prisoners. Seeking my salvation was the goal. I believed in God but could not feel his presence. This journey led me to the final battle against my gambling addiction. It was on for young and old.

THE AWAKENING

In the year 2007, a close friend introduced me to the teaching of Bruno Groening. A name I had never heard of. I started taking an interest in this teaching. I felt there was a divine truth behind it. There is a national conference twice a year. In November 2008, the group leader in Australia asked if anyone would like to help, please raise your hand. Somehow, I found my arm in a vertical position. How this happened is still a mystery to me.

On January 1st, 2009, I took a phone call from the Australian country leader. She casually asked me if I would still like to help. I said yes. Little did I know in which way I could help. She asked me if I would take on the task of Australian country treasurer. This sent a shiver down my spine. I felt like I had seen a ghost. Everything I had done concerning money was all in the safe I had built inside of me, never to be opened, the key in my possession.

Gambling had created many situations in my life that were my secret. I went bankrupt twice, leaving debts that I could not pay. I had family issues around inheritance. The cause is the rash life of a gambler. This is what I was faced with when I took the call. Silence reigned for about 30 seconds, and I responded, "I will call you back."

This was a sliding door moment for me. NO, the safe remains locked. YES, the contents are revealed. The beggar to be the CEO. He knows something that I don't know. He knew what was in the safe. The path to salvation was offered to me. I rang back, "Yes, and thank you." My first thoughts were, "Dear Bruno, please give me another chance with money."

MY INNER TRUTH REVEALED

I had been entrusted to take care of donations made from his friends from all over Australia. Transparency and order are essential. The ATO could audit us. Order was foreign territory for me.

A country treasurer and a gambler are not a good fit. The need to be relieved of my addiction was paramount. History says, "it is like drawing blood out of a stone." I had placed my last bet on a horse a few months before accepting this task. It was a thousand-dollar bet. Bruno Groening's teaching was becoming very real to me. He says, "Give me your worries, your burden. You don't know what to do with them." Now is my chance. I have had enough of the turmoil and the lying.

I followed his instructions, became calm in my chair, thought of something good, and then tuned in to him very strongly. From the bottom of my heart, I gave him my gambling addiction and immediately felt the peace. Then suddenly, I felt something leave me. I felt so light and free. I said to my nearby friend, "Something has left me. I feel so good."The foe had been captured, and a teacher had found the key.

I was finally released from prison and given a ticket to ride to my purpose, never looking back. I have never felt any compulsion to gamble, and the other spirits of competition also left me.

The Divine jewels of love and wisdom that had been smothered in my soul had the space to rise. The birdcage had been opened. I was free to be me.

The life of a country treasury in this organization has brought me so many gifts. The most important one was that money could be used in service. The money gathered from donations from friends all over the world was being used to pay for all the expenses accumulated, to bring his teaching to the world. Divine service was taking place.

Money used to be my master. It took charge of my life. Now I am the master of money, and I chose to use it in service to others, through my business.

This has changed my world. My purpose, I am putting into action. I could never have scripted the experiences I have had since making this decision. I am collaborating with organizations in Europe and Japan with my business, who are aligned with my goals in life, and that is to be a part of the New Age of bringing peace into the world and restoring the planet back into its divine condition.

Peace has replaced nervousness, love, instead of fear, a father who loves his sons, and a heart that is expanding daily. And I am very happy.

I have a family that extends into many countries. We are one is my conclusion. I have come a long way since my fiftieth birthday.

And I am so very grateful to God and Bruno Groening for believing in me, loving me, and rescuing me.

"Your inner purpose is to awaken. It is as simple as that. Finding and living in alignment with the inner purpose is the foundation for fulfilling your outer purpose. It is the basis for true success."

~ Eckhart Tole

CHAPTER ELEVEN

Being Human

By Sandra Elston

You are about to enter a memory. My memory. Of a lifetime lived thousands of years ago…

The scent of flowers drifted lazily across the warm evening air. In the sky, the stars were pinpricks of delight swirling and carpeting the velvety blackness of the sky. I could feel bubbles of excitement and happiness rising within me. I was wearing a new dress. It was blue and fitted me closely, showing off my figure. I felt pretty and happy. It was two weeks until my wedding and I was so excited.

I looked across the rooftop to the other guests. There were hibiscus bushes in planters that broke up the rooftop and created alcoves. Later in the season, the hibiscus blooms would be gathered as a valuable crop and dried to make tea, but for now, they were ornamental. The alcoves contained low tables and brightly colored gold and dark pink cushions. Candles flickered softly on the tables, creating an intimate feel even though I had been told that nearly two hundred guests would be attending the party. Servants circulated trays of delicious bite sized mezze. The fragrant scents of cinnamon, cumin, and cardamon mingled with the flowers.

Our hostess was the friend of my fiancé's parents and a woman of power and influence. Her annual birthday party was a significant event in the city's social calendar.

I was from a city which was a four hour ride to the North. Journeys of this length were difficult and dangerous, so they were rarely made. However, I had arrived three months ago with my parents after the negotiations for my marriage. As was the custom, they settled me at my fiancé's parent's house before returning home. My fiancé's parents were warm and welcoming. This was a good match for both families and everyone was keen to make it work.

I spent the next few months getting our new home set up and ready to live in before the wedding. There was a lot to do. We would be raising almost all of our food as was the custom. The kitchen garden had to be laid out and planted. Our chickens had arrived and would cluck and peck, keeping us company while we made our plans. The house was big. It had an estate attached to it that I hadn't even seen yet. There were twelve rooms to furnish, the kitchen to stock, and a nursery to get ready. It would undoubtedly have an occupant within a year.

We met with carpenters to design the furniture for our new home. I loved the preparations. It gave me time each day to get to know the man who would become my husband. The more I saw of him, the more I liked him. He was handsome, attentive, and funny. We enjoyed the same things and thought the same way. Together we were planning our life. The relationship was easy and comfortable. It had a familiarity, like putting on an old pair of slippers. almost as if we had met before. What started as an arranged marriage based on sound economics was flourishing into much more. I was so lucky!

I had been so busy with the house that I hadn't made any new friends, despite being in the city for three months. The party tonight was my chance to make friends and meet my neighbors.

During the course of the party, I was introduced to so many people I could hardly remember their names. We ate and danced, and I met new people. It was wonderful. I was going to like it here, I could tell. I loved to dance and afterward, my cheeks were flushed with excitement and exertion.

My fiancé was quite the catch. Five or six young women had hoped to marry him. I had been told that they were disappointed and envied me. However, when I met them, at the party they were lovely to me.

Towards the end of the evening, I was chatting with my fiancé and a friend of his. *A friend of ours now*, I reminded myself. There was a gentle hum of conversation around me. Then suddenly, the conversation seemed to falter and die. Finally, I looked up to see what had happened. A striking young woman dressed in yellows and gold with sleeves slashed to show off her arms stood at the entrance to the party. Her clothes were much brighter than any of the other women and she stood out sharply, making the other women appear dull in comparison. Glancing around the rooftop she seemed to be searching for something or someone. The other women were looking at her with disapproval while the men ignored her. Many of the guests seemed to know who and what she was – a prostitute. Prostitutes were never invited to parties. It just wasn't done.

I watched as she moved across the room until she seemed to see the person she was looking for. The bottom fell out of my stomach as she joined our group. She touched my fiancé on the arm and smiled at him. He took her by the hand and left, without so much as a look or a word to me. Like I was nothing. Yesterday's washing. I was stunned and embarrassed. I wished that the floor would swallow me up. Everyone was looking at me with a mixture of pity and curiosity. I didn't know what to do or where to look. What had started as a beautiful evening full of promise and delight, ended in disaster. My new life had ended in wreckage before it had even started. No one reached out to me. It was as if I was a leper and if they spoke to me my humiliation would be contagious. I was alone and isolated.

My stunned disbelief and shock deepened until I reached a catatonic state. I was taken home and gently put to bed as though I was an invalid. I didn't sleep. I lay still like a corpse. The questions raced through my mind. What does she have that I don't? Why does he want to be with her and not me? Why am I not enough? These questions whirled in my head for hours until my sense of not being enough burned deeply into my soul.

As dawn crept into the night sky, the shock began to lift. Waves of shame and rage crashed over me like a storm pounding the shoreline and consuming me completely. Then the tears came. They started as a trickle and became a torrent. I wept the bitter tears of humiliation.

Later that morning, I was in the sunny living room holding a pretty bowl in my hand, staring vacantly into space, miles away. The bowl was glazed blue on the outside and yellow on the inside. It fit nicely into my hand. As I was looking at it blankly, my fiancé breezed into the room with his easy smile as though nothing had happened. I threw it at him. Two more followed in rapid succession. The first two hit their mark, but he dodged the third. It was then that he realized that all was not right with his world. I couldn't believe it. He actually had to ask what was wrong. What was wrong with publicly humiliating me and leaving with a prostitute? He didn't see it.

As we talked, I felt a steely determination entering me. I wouldn't allow myself to be treated like this. I would live life on my own terms. I told him that I was breaking off our engagement and he laughed. It was unheard of. Our marriage contract had taken months of negotiation between our families. It was a finely balanced agreement setting out co-operation and collaboration between our family businesses and it was intended to last a lifetime. And then there was my dowry. He would have the right to keep it if I broke the contract. Without it, I would have no hope of marrying. I would become an old maid. Better that than a lifetime of being treated with contempt and a complete disregard for my feelings.

When he understood that I meant what I said, his good humor evaporated and was replaced with panic and desperation. It wouldn't just be me that was unpopular if this marriage contract was broken. His family was expecting closer ties with mine and the economic benefits that would bring. They had been at the party last night and had been as shocked as me by his behavior. I couldn't see a queue of young women waiting to replace me either after last night. Why would anyone volunteer for a life of contempt?

The realization that he had thrown away a lifetime with me for a matter of convenience dawned on him. We had been good together. Planning our life together had been fun. It had felt right. Now it was gone. When the enormity of his mistake dawned on him, he was sorry and pleaded to be forgiven.

We talked for hours. As we spoke, the dynamic of our relationship changed. It became equal. He was no longer in charge. We decided things together. I gained fierce independence that stayed with me. Some things in our relationship were not negotiable and if he wanted to stay with me, he would have to accept that. My requirement for marrying him was that he would be faithful to me. He agreed and he kept his promise. But so much trust had been destroyed. There was always a voice in the back of my mind wondering if he had played around. Wondering if I was enough for him, whether he wanted someone else.

I put away the vulnerable parts of me that day. I had been hurt so deeply that I vowed never to let that happen again. Better not to feel much than to feel like that! So I dialed down my ability to feel deep emotions to a level I could cope with. That allowed me to feel safe.

And so we were married two weeks later as planned.

The love between us grew as I had hoped it would. But the sense of not being enough stayed with me. It made me wonder if I was good enough, if he thought about looking around. My vulnerability also remained firmly hidden from that day forward. No way would I allow myself to be hurt like that again. I carried these deep wounds to my soul throughout that lifetime.

They have stayed with me ever since through each reincarnation, no matter the circumstances of that life or who I was with. Little nagging voices in the back of my head. "You are not enough." "You don't deserve him." "Why would he love you?" Carried from one lifetime to another through the centuries. Though it took me a long time to realize where they came from.

In the current times, I embarked on a path of healing these old wounds. As I did so, my Light team was giving help and insights along the way. One day I was shown that before I was born into that lifetime thousands of years ago, I had made a soul-level agreement with the man I became betrothed to. At a soul level, he wished to learn kindness. We both knew that it would take something big for this to happen. He asked my soul for help, and I agreed.

He needed to live it and feel it to embody it fully. The lesson worked and he learned how devastating a simple act of unkindness could be. He learned how to be kind and compassionate and he practiced this throughout our life together. This made me feel better, although I still think that maybe I need to have a bit of a word with myself about what my soul agrees to!

My Light team showed me that I had given my fiancé my power as a human being during the party. He had needed the extra help to learn kindness. I didn't even know that human beings had a power, let alone that I had given it away! I was shown that the power, or gift, of being human is to BE LOVE. To physically embody the vibration of love. I was told that it was time for me to reclaim this, which I did. I didn't feel any different, though, which was odd.

I was shown by the Light that I was still blocking feeling strong emotions to avoid being vulnerable. If I couldn't feel it, then it wouldn't hurt me. For this reason the gift could not function as the Light intended it to. Trauma was blocking the gift. As I cleared this, I felt love beginning to radiate through my body. I breathed the love deep into my belly and allowed it to spread into my blood, my bones, my organs, and my very being. The love grew as a golden light until it engulfed me. Every cell of my body radiated love and it felt wonderful. Now I know what it means to BE love. This is the gift of being human.

I am quite analytical as a person and reclaiming the gift of being human got me wondering. Were there other gifts or powers attached to other spiritual roles? So, I did what I do best and extrapolated the information that I had. If the gift of being human is to be love, to hold the vibration of love, what other roles may have gifts or powers? I had a massive amount of help from my Light team as I always do. They were brilliant, giving me insights and help along the way as I pondered this question. They gave me a list of spiritual functions that have power associated with them. The roles are:

Being Human
Priest/Priestess/Nun
High Priest/Priestess
Saint
Angel
Archangel
Ascended Master
Spiritual Teacher
Seraphim
Demi-God/Goddess
God/Goddess

In addition to these roles, some people have a connection with the elementals. These do not carry power, but they bring awesome knowledge and wisdom. A link to the elementals is a great blessing. The elementals are:

Earth
Wind
Water
Air

I'm not sure this is a complete list, but it is plenty to go with. It is within my nature to push the boundaries of what I know so I went through the list and checked which of these roles I had carried out. Then I checked whether the power was with me. If yes, was it also working as intended? Lightworkers have experienced a lot of traumatic situations over their lifetimes. Trauma can dim your Light and make you doubt yourself.

I would like to show you that you can go through this same process if you wish to, to find out which spiritual roles you have undertaken and whether the gifts and power from those roles are with you. This is not an academic exercise for the interest of it. If you are reading this then the chances are that this is not the first time you have incarnated on the Earth. As part of the training, you are likely to have accepted one or more spiritual roles. This is how you learned and were prepared for this lifetime. These roles have power attached to them. It is time for you to reconnect with these gifts and powers. They are the tools that you will be needing to carry out your work in this lifetime.

I can almost hear you thinking, "Well, that's all very lovely, but I've got no idea which roles I may have taken on."

You know which roles you have taken on – or at least your energy does. I am going to show you how to access the wisdom that you hold within you.

I am an Energy Alignment Method (EAM) Mentor and in EAM we use a tool called the sway to access your inner wisdom. It's a form of muscle testing similar to how a kinesiologist tests for allergies. To use the sway, stand up with your knees soft. The sway can be used to answer yes or no questions. Ask yourself a question to which you know the answer, such as your name or favorite color. The questions don't need to be deep and meaningful to test if your sway works. You will sway forwards or backward in response to your question. Try it again with another question you know the answer to so that you can find out which direction is yes, and which is no. Once you can use your sway, you will be able to use it to find out what is true in your energy which is absolutely awesome.

It is important to ensure no energetic gunk is around to skew the response so you get an accurate answer from your energy on any subject. If you have resistance on a subject, you can easily get an incorrect answer about what is true in your energy which is really unhelpful. For instance, if you fear water and you swayed on whether you should stay by a lake, the answer may will be a 'no' even if it is the best thing for you. In this case once you have released the fear of water then the answer is likely to change to a 'yes'. So, to ensure that you get an accurate answer from your energy, it is essential to ensure there is no dense energy around creating resistances or negative emotions.

It is very common to have mazing over the question of which spiritual roles you have undertaken. I certainly did! Mazing just makes it really unclear what the answer is on a subject and everything gets muddled up – hence the name. So before you start, it is essential to check for this and clear it if it's there.

Say the following question aloud and check what answer your sway gives you. It's imperative to use these exact words as sometimes things can get hidden.

"Do I have mazing of any designation and any tier over which spiritual roles I have undertaken?"

Then, if your sway is a 'no,' you are ready to start.

If your sway is a 'yes,' you will need to clear the mazing before starting. To do this, please say the release phrase:

"I am ready to release this mazing of any designation and any tier over which spiritual roles I have undertaken. I release and let it go now and send it back to the Light with love, in all forms on all levels and at all points in time."

Repeat this phrase three times, each time taking a deep, cleansing breath to help let go of the resistance. Check with your sway to make sure the mazing has been released. If not, please repeat the release statement until the mazing is fully removed.

Now you are ready to access your inner wisdom. This is so simple. Please start at the top of the list and sway on whether it applies to you for each spiritual role. For instance, 'I am an angel' and see whether you get a yes or a no. Don't be worried if the answer surprises you. Just go through the list and record your answers. When checking, please remember that you may not always incarnate in the same gender that you are now.

If you wish to do so, you may find it helpful to complete the grid below.

Once you have done this, it's time to look at the other questions. These are:

Is your power with you?

Is your power working as it is intended to by the Light?

Again, just go through the list and record your answers without judgment. Then, once you have a completed grid, look at your

answers. It will tell you where you are in the process. How absolutely amazing is that?

Have you undertaken this Spiritual Role? Y/N	Is the power with you? Y/N	Is the power working as it is intended to? Y/N
Being Human		
Priest/Priestess/Nun		
High Priest/Priestess		
Saint		
Angel		
Archangel		
Ascended Master		
Spiritual Teacher		
Seraphim		
Demi-God/Goddess		
God/Goddess		

Do you have a connection to the Elementals? Y/N	Is the connection with you? Y/N	Is the connection working as it is intended to? Y/N
Earth		
Wind		
Water		
Air		

Embodying the Gift of Being Human

Love is the birth right of every person on this planet. It is what makes us human. Awakening to that truth is incredibly special. Allowing yourself to embody love at a physical level, to become the vibration of love, allowing love to be your guiding light as you navigate life is the greatest gift that you can give yourself.

I asked the Goddesses of Love to help me and five Goddesses agreed and stepped forward. They have decided to provide a meditation to embody the gift and power of being human. The power of being a human being is extraordinary. It is the power to **be** love. To embody the vibration of love in every cell of your body. How beautiful is that?

Please take a seat somewhere where you won't be disturbed. If you would like, please light a candle or some incense.

Ask the Archangel Sandalphon to ground you thoroughly.

Ask the Archangel Michael to place his royal blue cloak of protection over you so that only energy for the highest and greatest good can reach you, leave you or come through you.

Ask to connect to the highest vibration of love you can join right now. See it as pure golden Light, shining incredibly brightly. Connect to this love, this bright shining golden Light. Feel the vibration of the love. It is high, pure and clear. Revel in it.

Breathe it into your belly, taking slow deep breaths. Keep doing this until your belly feels filled with love. Then transfer your attention to your base chakra. This is at the bottom of your spine, where your pelvic floor is. Breathe the love into your pelvic floor, allowing it to spread throughout the whole of your base chakra. Your base chakra contains your survival instincts. If you have fears about money, somewhere to live, having enough, this is where they live. These fears are limiting and can cause us to contract into defensive behavior, protecting what we have at any cost. Love knows that there is plenty. That everyone who can accept prosperity will receive it.

So, breathe the pure golden love deep into your base chakra. Allow yourself to rise above survival. Allow yourself to receive prosperity. Allow yourself to relax in the golden glow of the love you are breathing in. Allow it to grow and expand. Breathing it in so that your base chakra expands, filled with pure golden love. Allow your base chakra to encapsulate your whole body, knowing that there is plenty for everyone. There always has been and there always will be. We just need to allow ourselves to connect with the flow of abundance and receive it. Breathing it in.

Allow your attention to move to your legs and feet and breathe the love into them. This will ground the love into your physical existence. Breathing it in, allowing it to expand and flow through you.

Move your attention to your Earth Star chakra. This is about 15 cm below your feet. The Earth Star chakra holds the seeds of your potential. Breathe the pure golden love into your Earth Star chakra. Allow the pure golden love to flow into your Earth Star chakra, filling it with this beautiful energy and filling your potential with pure golden love. Breathe it in and allow it to flow and expand until the chakra is full.

Once your Earth Star chakra, legs, Base chakra, and belly are filled with love, allow the pure golden love to spread up your torso into your arms, hands, and chest. Filling them with pure golden love. Allow the love to move up your neck and into your spine. Breathe it into them. Breathe it into your face and head. Breathing it in.

Once your physical body is filled with pure golden Light, bring your attention to your etheric body, which exists as a thin layer right next to your physical body. Breathe the pure golden love into your etheric body. Breathing it in and allowing it to flow, relaxing and enjoying the vibration of love as it fills you up.

Allow the golden cloud of love to expand into the emotional layer of your energy. Breathe it through and enjoy the expansion, allowing it to flow through you and fill you up, breathing it in.

Bring your focus to the spiritual layer of your energy and breathe the pure golden love into it. Allow the energy to flow and expand into every layer of your spiritual body, enjoying the feeling of love, and soaking up the vibration. Keep breathing the pure golden love through your energy bodies until they are filled with love.

Allow yourself to rest in the energy as it integrates and becomes part of you.

When you are ready, wiggle your toes, stretch and open your eyes.

Know that you can access this feeling whenever you want to.

Epilogue

I would like you to imagine a world where everyone has fully embodied their gift as a human being, that they have fully embodied love. Imagine how that would affect their decisions – the way they choose to live their lives. Love has the potential to permeate everything: each person, every aspect of their lives and every corner of the planet. People would choose from a place of plenty, knowing that they could afford to be generous and kind because there is enough for everyone. They could do work that they found fulfilling and fun while still living well. They would choose leaders that reflect their values and ideals and bring harmony to the world. This is a potential future for our planet and could be our legacy to the next generation. We can choose it and build it with one person at a time, embodying the gift of being human—awakening to love.

"Don't fear the light within. May it ignite the sacred flame in your soul."

~ Paulo Coelho

CHAPTER TWELVE

Free at Last

By John Spender

In the middle of a busy day in his landscaping business, Akmal was driving to his next job. He had an afternoon of back-to-back appointments; work was busy and he had hardly any time to himself. He had been going through some personal struggles after his girlfriend of eight years had run off with his cousin. He felt confused, angry and sad at the betrayal. Life felt so unfair. It was tearing him apart, and his family too. How could his cousin do that? They had grown up together. Akmal's mom was from Los Angeles, her parents and both their parents were from the big town. You didn't come across that so often these days. Most people came from other states or from other countries, like his dad. He had migrated to the US from Karachi, Pakistan when he was 19 as a student and decided to stay.

Akmal had had his business for almost 11 years. He was based in the Bay area, near LAX airport, and he lived nearby in Redondo Beach. His father said the difficult feelings he was experiencing were rooted in jealousy and encouraged Akmal to feel the pain. Be with the hurt of the loss and allow it to break you open to feel more so as not to become bitter, his dad would say. Eventually, feeling lost and willing to try anything, Akmal found the support of a Reiki master and meditation teacher. She helped Akmal to let go of the story, to go within and connect with his higher self, building his self-esteem in the process. He discovered that when one feels lost and hurt, it's better to take action towards healing yourself rather than sitting with the pain for too long. He joined a meditation group, which helped him to live in the present moment, tap into his intuition and connect with his spirit guides.

"You are what you are and what you are is a spark of God force and that God force is all compassion and forgiveness."
~ Stuart Wilde

One of the patterns that Akmal had developed to avoid the pain was throwing himself into work, and as he got out of the car and walked up the drive towards the next house, he heard someone say, "If you are not careful, you will be in a serious accident." He turned around, but no-one was there. Strange, the voice had sounded so real. Akmal wondered if it was the aftereffects of the bottle of expensive wine that he had drunk last night. But as the day went on he forgot about it and enjoyed the late summer sun that daylight savings brought. On his way home, he decided to drive to the liquor store. He went to turn left, waiting for the car on the opposite side of the road to turn right as indicated. At this moment, reality slowed down, Akmal's awareness acutely heightened to his surroundings, taking in the sunny evening. The atmosphere on the streets was buzzing with summer vibes; people were dining at the sidewalk cafes and walking back and to the beach. It didn't feel like 7:30pm. The one thing that stood out above everything else was a hot blonde in a bikini walking down the footpath to the beach.He saw the man with his blinker on staring at the woman miss his turn and come straight for Akmal's pick-up. Instantly, Akmal jumped on the horn and the guy, white-faced, sprang into action, missing Akmal's truck by a whisker. Akmal remained still, looking in his rear vision mirror to see if the guy had stopped, but he kept going. That was the evening Akmal awakened to the power of the supernatural, a world beyond our five senses.

Over the previous six months, he had become less passionate about his business, especially after his previous five-week vacation the winter just gone. The last time he felt like this was a few years back after he had almost worked himself into an early grave. His mom often told him, "You need a holiday." and, "At the end of your life, you will never wish you had worked more." Every year since then, he had taken a five-week vacation in the winter and two weeks at Christmas. After a few years of this routine, he found he felt empty inside when he returned from his holiday. The recent double betrayal compounded this feeling. Why had he attracted this situation into his life? He would ask himself. The answer came back that he needed to become more available to the people that matter in his life. He desired a meaningful life. Landscaping had been all he ever knew. His business was safe and predictable. His dad said he was missing a sense of fulfillment. He said he went through the same emptiness before he decided to sell his chain of restaurants and retire. He suggested that Akmal create a lifestyle business that he didn't need a break from. His dad thought an online business would suit his son's adventurous spirit and give him something else to focus on other than the breakup. Akamal mentioned that he had enough wealth to retire, but his dad warned him that at 34, he would quickly become bored.

The conversation with his dad had Akmal thinking about his future. He knew he needed a change of career, but what would that look like? Eventually, to try to make up his mind, he decided to go headfirst into the personal development scene, attending a different seminar almost every weekend. He also signed up for a year-long training program to become a life coach. Slowly, he felt the emptiness begin to ebb away, giving birth to hope for the future by putting his attention on helping others. As part of the life coaching program, the group of aspiring coaches went through two intense NLP programs. On the first day, as Akmal entered the room, he was initially filled with excitement for the adventure that awaited. The trainer, Mike, prefaced his expectations as well as the seminar rules. Mike's confidence and knowledge of NLP set the stage for five days of transformation. The first hurdle came on the first night when the group met in the parking lot for a surprise breakthrough session. When Akmal learned that the group was going to put out fire with their mouths, he panicked and his brain automatically came up with excuses so fast he broke out in a sweat. But, there was no way out. If he didn't complete the challenge, he would fail the course.

Akmal wasn't the kind of person that liked losing, let alone failing, but a childhood memory had a powerful hold of him. When Mike asked if anyone was afraid of fire like a phobia, Akmal spoke up rather than suffer in silence. In front of everyone, Mike asked him what had happened to make him feel that way. Akmal told Mike about how when he was five, playing on their grandparent's ranch, he and his elder cousin had been messing around with fire. They were melting bottles on sticks, watching the plastic melt, dripping to the ground, when his cousin anciently flicked some of the melting plastic onto Akmal's face. It sizzled on his skin. He overcame unbearable agony and ran like a child possessed, screaming his head off, toward the ranch house. His grandma, hanging the clothes out to dry, heard Akmal and saw him sprinting toward the house. She figured the boys had been playing by the burning cleanup stack and instinctively grabbed a bucket of water as she ran towards her grandson. She could see that he had a burnt face even from 70 yards away. Once they reached each other, his grandma made Akmal stick his head in the bucket of cold water. She put his head under the cold shower at the ranch as he sobbed at the shock and pain.

*"We cannot create a new future by
holding onto emotions of the past."*
~ Dr. Joe Dispenza

Luckily, Akmal's grandmother had acted quickly and as a result, today, he has a small scar the size of the nail of his pinky finger on his left cheek. But the emotional scarring had never left him. That night, Mike took him through an induction to release the trauma forever. Mike firmly and calmly spoke with Akmal. "Is it okay that you shift your phobia tonight at a deep subconscious level and for you to be consciously aware of it?" Akmal nodded and said, "Yes" in a clear voice as he closed his eyes. Mike said to Akmal, "Imagine you are in a large movie theatre with a giant white screen at the front. Now, see what you saw. Hear what you heard, and feel the feelings you felt as you project the memory of burning your face onto the large screen. Can you do that for me?" With his eyes still closed, Akmal nodded. Mike said, "That's right! Instead of color, I want you to make the screen black and white. Do you know the old black and white TVs with the static? "Yes," said Akmal. "Add some static to the screen and play the memory of you being burned up on the screen. Can you do that?" continued Mike. Akmal nodded confirmation again as Mike asked him to rewind the story, then fast forward, pause, then play again, then rewind, and on they went for another two minutes, playing with the story in Akmal's mind. Mike had taken Akmal through the fast phobia model, scrambling the significant emotional event, deleting the trigger and his attachment to the experience.

Mike then asked Akmal how much fear he had towards the burning torch. Akmal stared at the flame and calmly answered a four. Mike then proceeded to take him through a swish pattern, helping Akmal bring the image of him being afraid of the fire and then an image of him not being afraid of the flame. Mike then had Akmal switch them back and forward quickly before finishing with the picture of him being scared and having him shatter the memory into a million pieces. Finally, Mike guided him to walk over the broken glass in his mind towards the image of him not being afraid of the fire.

When Mike tested him, there was minimal fear present and he felt unstoppable. Everyone cheered and clapped and of course, Akmal had to go first. All the other coaches were chanting "Akmal, Akmal, Akmal!" You would never believe that 32 people could be that loud. Akmal slapped his chest with his right first and pumped his other hand in the air like John Travolta in *Saturday Night Fever*. Mike handed him the flaming torch, the fire flickering only inches from his face, the feeling of excitement tingled all over his body as Akmal held the torch above his head as instructed, tilting his head back, mouth open wider than the Golden Gate Bridge, exhaling before placing the flame in his mouth. His eyes bulged out of their sockets, his mouth closed around the flame to the gasps of his peers. Starved of oxygen, the fire was instantly extinguished. Akmal pulled the torch out of his mouth, punching the blackened head of the torch in the air as the cheers and whistles echoed across the parking lot. He was floating on cloud nine as Mike gave him a solid bear hug before he returned to the circle of high-fiving and backslapping coaches. Mike was also beaming with excitement. He gave a speech about the stories we tell ourselves relating to things that happened to us in the past, creating a future that isn't a reflection of our unlimited potential. We live a lie that holds us back from living life to the fullest. Ultimately, when we challenge these beliefs or falsehoods, we clear a path for an empowering paradigm of possibility where we begin to trust our decisions.

"Becoming awake involves seeing our confusion more clearly."
~ Rumi

Mike called the next participant up as Akmal processed what just happened. It felt like a quantum leap of truth, banishing the lie that had always lurked there in the back of his mind. But, Akmal thought to himself, it's one thing to know the truth and it's a completely different experience to live it. He felt it was like finally breaking iron chains that turn to dust the moment they were tested. People go to their graves strangled by the past, never having dared to live their life. We all know that the past doesn't have to determine the future, but how many are actually living that truth, Akmal pondered. The shell of his old reality was breaking apart into a new world, one to embrace, not to fear as his peer Tony passed him his Zippo lighter with a smile. Akmal laughed, no longer afraid to pop the top and flick the flame. Martin Luther King's words flickered in his mind: "Free at last, free at last." Akmal had experienced emancipation at a soul level that will never affect him again in this life or any lives he may have in the future. That warmed his being like the sun on a frosty morning. Mike had finished the third breakthrough with one of the women, who also didn't like the idea of putting fire in her mouth. You could tell the experience had also been transformational for her. The trainer gave another speech about not being naive to think that one big breakthrough doesn't mean you won't have any more breakthroughs to confront. He continued stating that this breakthrough was a reminder that every one of us has what it takes to face adversity, awakening our unlimited potential in the process.

The truth Akmal gained from this challenge helped him know that anything is possible, and the experience would serve him well for the terrible phone call that he received soon after from his mom. She was emotional and could barely speak without crying and sobbing as she babbled out that Akmal's dad had been in a severe car accident. Later, when Akmal quietly entered the room, his mom sat next to his dad, holding his hand. Tears sprang instantly to his eyes. His dad was in an induced coma, allowing the brain to rest and heal from his serious injuries. Akmal couldn't believe it. His dad had finally awakened to his passion for living life to the fullest after 30 years of working himself to the bone in his chain of restaurants. In retirement, his dad had taken up painting, becoming quite good, showing his pieces around the country. He also regularly practiced Brazilian Jiu-Jitsu and was already a blue belt. His dad's relationship with Akmal's mom had risen to another level of happiness, regularly traveling overseas with little or no arguing. Now his dad was in a critical condition. The doctors were giving him a 20% chance of survival and even if he made it, he would have permanent brain damage. Memories came flooding back about the life of his grandfather, or dada (Urdu for granddad), as he affectionately called him. His grandfather had worked his entire life to provide for his family. At least his dad had ten good years of living life the way he wanted. Akmal was even more determined to create a life that he didn't need to take a break from, where every day was as fulfilling as the next. Sometimes the truth that we seek is wrapped in pain, hurt and adversity, but Akmal was discovering good things can emerge from bad experiences. Awakening to who we are is a character-building experience that evolves one's soul, like a plastic band stretched to its limits, never restored to its original size.

"The possibilities are numerous once
we decide to act and not react."
~ George Bernard Shaw

Akmal convinced his mother to go home and rest after being in the room for almost 48 hours. She looked like a zombie. They both agreed that a good night's sleep would help her worry less, because worrying wouldn't change anything. Akmal quietly sat next to his father and prayed silently, picturing healing light entering his dad's body as his Reiki master had taught him. She had also told him the body had everything it needed to heal; all we do is create the right environment to foster that healing. After his experience at the traffic lights, Akmal knew angels existed. He realized that awakening to your inner truth and unlimited potential is a multidimensional, often chaotic process, one that re moves the veil of lies, self-sabotaging patterns, limiting beliefs and lack of any kind. Making way for clarity, a sense of mission, purpose, an abundance mindset, and unlimited potential. Step by step, anything is possible, thought Akmal as he sent healing energy to his father, surrendering to the intense warm flow that seemed to be coming from a divine presence. The energy felt like love, pouring down from above, channeling through his body and the hand holding his dad's. After twenty minutes, Akmal opened his eyes and saw his dad in front of him, as though in perfect health. Akmal couldn't speak; he and looked up at the clock, and was astonished to see he had been channeling for over an hour. He felt energized, fulfilled with a sense of knowing that his dad would live through this tragic accident as tears of joy rolled down his cheeks.

Akmal now saw the betrayal he had experienced when his girlfriend ran off with his cousin as a drop in the ocean compared to the prospect of losing his father. The shift in perspective was massive, and after attending countless personal development events, he was ready to move on. Having a deep connection and relationship with himself enabled him to release his past traumas and focus on what he wanted from the future. His parents needed him now more than ever, and Akmal was glad he could be there for them. Before the accident, his dad had told him never to underestimate the strength of his soul. It has bounced back for lifetimes. He prayed that his father's soul was strong enough to recover from this tragedy. Two weeks later, his dad had awakened from his coma and although he could not speak clearly because of his injuries, the doctors called his consciousness a miracle. The next day, Akmal received a call from Mike to offer him a position on his coaching team. The exciting news came as a shock – he had only just finished the program. To say he was over the moon was an understatement. He couldn't wait to share the news with his dad. Akmal chose to speak to his dad as if he was already healed, even though he wouldn't be able to respond. It would be months before his dad was able to form any sort of speech at all.

Akmal was beginning to transcend the duality of emotions, allowing them to flow through him rather than attach a story to them. He felt an inner knowing that to live truthfully we are constantly dying to old patterns and paradigms birthing new realities to experience many times in one life. A steady flow of death and rebirth. What was once true for Akmal as a child was completely different for him as a teenager. What he believed to be true as a young adult was poles apart from what he knew to be true as a middle aged man. So it is for everybody; if you are not evolving, you are open to life forcing you to yield to your transformation. As Akmal arrived for the first day of working with Mike, he saw the next group of people gathered, waiting to transform, and he felt the words of Martin Luther King echoing in his mind, "Free at last, free at last."

"Dip into your own soul. Find your own truth. What calls to your heart. What moves your spirit. Make your life dance to the song of your own essence."

~ Diana Haymond

Author Biographies

Casey Plouffe
CHAPTER ONE

Casey Plouffe is a passionate, forward-thinking business woman, pastor of Church of Sovereign Temples, and an inspiring leader in the Divine Feminine Christ movement that's currently sweeping the planet. From nursing, to becoming a million-dollar network marketer, to investing in million-dollar real estate properties, to running a non-traditional church welcoming all names of divinity, Casey now leads a global movement guiding humanity back to a path of personal inner communion with God, encouraging individuals to embody their own sovereign divinity. Using the First Amendment of the U.S. Constitution as the foundation, part of Casey's church mission is to protect its members from medical tyranny and viral programming, while healing war consciousness. Casey is steadfast in educating others on how to connect with their inner truth to heal past trauma, addiction, and command miracles through the ascension process.

If you are interested in Casey's 13-week guided sacred online journey gathering to connect with your inner truth and directly mentor with ascended masters of light, visit www.sophiacodecir-cleministry.com to schedule an interview.

If you are interested in learning more about Casey's breath and elements retreats or you'd like to learn more about her wellness opportunity and consuming high quality nutrients to enhance your personal inner communion,
email SovereignTemples@gmail.com.

Attend Church of Sovereign Temples' weekly virtual inner communion gatherings by joining the mailing list at STofGod.org.

If you or anyone you love is seeking help to cure alcoholism or Alcohol Overuse Disorder, visit www.powerfuldrinking.com.

Anne Henning
CHAPTER TWO

Anne Henning graduated with a Master's degree in Spiritual Psychology. In 2018 she co-founded *I Choose Soul*, a platform that spreads an abundance mindset through spiritual based techniques. Anne's greatest gift is the ability to nurture and support those on their spiritual journey.

A 15-yearlong oncology nursing career shaped Anne's desire to treat the whole person, beyond the body, to include the mind and spirit. During her career, she became a supervisor and assisted the integrative therapy team to introduce holistic therapy in the hospital setting. As the Nurse Practice Council Chair, Anne expanded a multifaceted self-care program to all healthcare personnel.

In response to the recent mass exodus of nurses and work-related fatigue, Anne developed a restorative retreat specifically designed for nurses to replenish the whole self. The retreat blueprint allows participants to be exposed to a vast range of healing modalities. Nurses are assisted with a transformation that brings them from burnout to creating a vibrant life full of joy.

Anne chooses to inspire people to live their best life by living her own life to the fullest. Her greatest bliss is found working alongside her mother to promote a medical device they invented together. This simple device is known as the Beata Clasp, and it works to ease the nurse's daily frustration of tangled tubing. This is a legacy her mother is proud to leave behind, and Anne hopes she, too, can leave a lasting spiritual legacy in the lives of many nurses.

www.ichoosesoul.com

Andrew Geldert
CHAPTER THREE

Andrew was an underworld figure who become involved in the outlaw motorcycle club lifestyle which almost cost him his life after being shot twice at close range in a bikie barroom brawl. His life was bought undone after he became the target of an undercover Police operation that resulted in a seven-year prison sentence and him being declared a drug trafficker for his involvement in an international cocaine dealing syndicate.

During his incarceration he worked through his trauma after coming to realize that he had become the product of his broken childhood. Andrew set about turning his life around and began a disciplined approach to balance himself mentally, physically, and spiritually, and completed three Diplomas and a Bachelor of Business Degree.

Since being released from prison in 2017 Andrew has transformed his life and perspectives, fulfilled corporate Senior Management roles, and later connected to his passion and purpose by completing certifications in holistic health and wellbeing and is now a Personal Development and Transformational Coach, Energetic Practitioner and Keynote Speaker.

A finalist in the Most Inspirational Man of the Year at the Men in Black – Mates in Construction Ball 2021 State Function, Andrew is the host of the soon to be released "Man to Man – Let's Talk About It" men's mental health and wellbeing podcast series, the founder of the men's support group the Man to Man Brotherhood Movement, co-author of the soon to be released Moments in Time and author of 'How to Find Hope and Heal Yourself'.

Angela Orora Medway-Smith
CHAPTER FOUR

Angela Orora Medway-Smith is a spiritual channel, author and teacher, master healer, Life & Soul Alignment Coach and retreat leader from Wales.

Her business is called Cariad Spiritual and she works both in person and online, spreading the light at workshops, festivals and retreats all over the world.

Holistic healing is her passion; she's set up healing clinics, created spiritual festivals and holistic events, trained hundreds of healers and given thousands of clients worldwide guidance from spirit.

Angela helped found Divine Energy International, a worldwide membership non-profit for energy healers. Its vision is 'a world where divine energy is for all.' She's on a mission! Changing the world one person at a time.

She devotes her life to awakening divine souls like you to their potential and believes that we all have the ability to transform, to emerge from the chrysalis of this human life, to 'Be The Butterfly' and SOAR; developing a deep connection to our soul, aligning with our true destiny.

Angela is incredibly blessed to be a direct channel to the Ascended Master and Angelic Collectives and has published her channeled books 'The Book of Many Colours' and 'The Book of Many Flames'. She is co-author of the #1 Amazon Best Sellers, Strong Mothers and 25 Tools for Goddesses: Volume 4 of the Wellness Universe Ultimate Guide to Self-Care.

Angela offers spiritual consultations, Life & Soul Alignment Coaching, women's retreats, healing, healer and intuitive development training worldwide.

Connect with Angela at https://www.cariadspiritual.com/

Helle Lisle
CHAPTER FIVE

Helle Lisle is living in the countryside in Denmark together with her husband. They have two grown-up sons who brings a lot of happiness to their life.

In 2018 Helle founded Heart based Life – a business where she is devoted to teach personal development and inspire people to live their life aligned with the wisdom of the heart and with their true values and highest potential.

Originally Helle wasa medical doctor and a psychiatrist and had her own clinic for ten years. She also has a wide range of therapeutic educations and is a mindfulness teacher. Over the last years her focus has been on studying compassion, gratitude, heart intelligence and the work of visionary people like Joe Dispenza, Lynne McTaggert, Eckhart Tolle, and Marci Shimoff.

As a therapist she has studied and implemented numerous modalities to help support her client's highest quality of life. Helle loves learning and growing and is very passionate about sharing her knowledge, wisdom and perspective with her clients.

Helle works with individuals and groups and teaching workshops and retreats.

Her area of expertise are in the field on compassion, mindfulness, meditation and heart intelligence. Helle is eager to teach and inspire people to realize that it is possible to transform old limiting beliefs, habits and mindsets and start living a life aligned with our inner truth.

Helle is also the author of two books written in Danish: "Mindfulness & Compassion" from 2020 and "My grateful heart" from 2021.

For more information:
www.heartbasedlife.com

Grit Sanders
CHAPTER SIX

Grit Sanders was born and raised in Copenhagen, Denmark. As the former part-owner and creative director of the children's clothing company, Cosy Design, she was taken over by the passion for photography, art and now writing. She creates unique vivid photographic artworks under the name Portrait Tales. When travelling the world as an adventurer with her large format camera she takes soulful portraits of people and tribes far for her Authentic Tales series. Lately Grit has begun writing her Story Tales about spiritual growth and personal development, believing we all have unique gifts and talents and as we emerge with life, rewrite our paradigms, we create a unique pattern where we get to express our life, our joy, our sorrow, our love.

Driven by a strong resilience she believes that if you nurture your passion and participate in life with your gift - the more you share this joy ... the more you will encourage others to fulfill their dreams.

We can all make a difference by entering our call.

Grit now resides in the northern part of Copenhagen enjoying her creative workspace, where the fusion of light, canvas, and brush form the aura surrounding Story Tales, Portrait Tales, and Authentic Tales.

It's much more than a portrait - It's your story. It's poetry.

WWW.GRITSANDERS.COM
Email: sanders@gritsanders.dk
Facebook: www.Facebook.com/gritsanders
Instagram: www.Instagram.com/gritsanders

Suzie Curiel
CHAPTER SEVEN

Suzie Curiel considers herself a Southern California native, residing in the Inland Empire since the age of 5. She has a B.A. degree from The University of California Riverside where she double majored in Psychology and Spanish. She was an educator for several years before obtaining her License in Real Estate. She loves being a Realtor because it allows her the opportunity to help individuals, couples and families achieve their dreams in everything Real Estate related. She shares that nothing compares to the joy of observing a person's facial expression of happiness and fulfillment when their home sale or purchase has manifested. She's also an advocate for helping stray dogs and cats by providing food and shelter and connecting them to foster organizations. Since she was in elementary school, she has enjoyed writing as an outlet of self expression and storytelling. Although she's new to this writing space, she's grateful and humbled by the experience.

JeNeil Miles
CHAPTER EIGHT

JeNeil Miles is something of a modern-day renaissance man that has expanded his artistic mind into all that he does: from working multiple jobs, various types of writing, and having soulful conversations with a diverse amount of people. JeNeil is also a passionate Hip-Hop artist that goes by the moniker Balance Universal.

JeNeil was born and raised in Mobile, Alabama, and immediately gravitated to all kinds of entertainment. From his first performance on stage at the age of four, he would find himself in front of many more crowds doing plays, dancing, speaking, rapping, singing, and teaching. When he neared adulthood, he joined the military and served for twelve years. After realizing the military life was not for him, he left with an honorable discharge to seek out a life that brought him more fulfillment.

JeNeil now resides near the beaches of Gulf Shores, AL. He enjoys collaborating with other artists on music projects, playing basketball, and taking lengthy walks at various parks. JeNeil is quite known in the small town he resides in, and has a laugh that brings joy to the hearts of many.

Ivan Budiani
CHAPTER NINE

Ivan is a lover of her life, her parent's pride and joy, and a limitless dreamer of her own reality. She is a cheerful girl who loves books, yoga, and nature. She completed her 200-hour yoga certification in 2019 and has been a yoga practitioner for four years.

She was born in 1995 in Bali, Indonesia. She completed her Bachelor's degree in English for Education in one of the universities in North Bali. She has been an aspiring writer since she was younger. She loved reading and writing children's stories when she was in elementary school. Then, she started to write fictional short stories as a teenager. One day she decided that she needs to write more about herself and her life.

Along with her chapter in this book, she wants to encourage you to be true to yourself, to be your own person, and to take full charge of your own happiness.

You can reach her at:
Email: niluhivanbudiani@gmail.com
Instagram/ Facebook: Ivan Budiani

Hugh Dinning
CHAPTER TEN

Hugh Dinning has been a businessman for most of his working years. He had a profound experience while hiking in a forest in the Muir Woods National Monument. He arrived at the entrance of the forest depressed and totally exhausted. After 15 minutes of walking amongst the powerful trees and listening to the sounds of water running over sandstone rocks, his body was suddenly full of life, joy, and clarity. This experience opened a love for nature and deep respect for its power. A new business was born, based on sustainability, fueled by serving.

His business is founded on replacing plastic bags with bags made from organic fabrics. Having a background in textiles, he is educating people on how to shop and store bags, using these eco-friendly fabrics that are practical, beautiful, and help restore the planet. All printing and dying of colors are from plants, flowers, and herbs. All waste products, go out to feed the neighboring plantations.

He now has a fire in his belly to unite business and ecology. That business can be an instrument of change.

And a passion to bring children out of the material world and connect them with nature.

He loves hiking, writing poems, and actively helps an organization in the field of help and healing on the spiritual path, through the teaching of Bruno Groening.

You can reach him
hugh@thekeeper.earth
+61412359011
Website: https://thekeeper.earth/

Sandra Elston
CHAPTER ELEVEN

Sandra left a successful corporate career after thirty years and became a healer.

This sounds like a massive change but the truth is that the need to change her life crept up on Sandra slowly. For a long time she loved her work. Then it was OK. Then really it wasn't OK at all. And in the background her life purpose had been calling to her, softly at first and then louder and louder. Until it reached the point where every day she woke up knowing that she was in the wrong job.

So in 2011 Sandra left the corporate world. She retrained first in Reiki and then as a crystal healer (best excuse to buy crystals ever!). Then she found the Energy Alignment Method, or more likely it found her. Sandra was trained personally by Yvette Taylor, the creator of the Energy Alignment Method and is one of the first 50 accredited EAM Mentors globally.

Being Human is the story of Sandra's awakening to the gift and power of Being Human.

There are free resources, including a recording of the meditation and a workbook to help you to use the information in your life. To download them please visit:
www.sandraelston.com/Being_Human

Sandra lives in Dorset with her family and loves going to the beach.

John Spender
CHAPTER TWELVE

John Spender is a 27-time International Best Selling co-author, who didn't learn how to read and write at a basic level until he was ten years old. He has since traveled the world, started many businesses leading him to create the best-selling book series A Journey Of Riches. He is an Award Winning International Speaker and Movie Maker.

John worked as an international NLP trainer and has coached thousands of people from various backgrounds through all sorts of challenges. From the borderline homeless to very wealthy in- dividuals, he has helped many people to get in touch with their truth to create a life on their terms.

John's search for answers to living a fulfilling life has taken him to work with Native American Indians in the Hills of San Diego, in the forests of Madagascar, swimming with humpback whales in Tonga, exploring the Okavango Delta of Botswana and the Great Wall of China. He's traveled from Chile to Slovakia, Hun- gary to the Solomon Islands, the mountains of Italy and the streets of Mexico.

Everywhere his journey has taken him, John has discovered a hunger among people to find a new way to live, with a yearning for freedom of expression. His belief that everyone has a book in them was born.

He is now a writing coach, having worked with more than 200 authors from 40 different countries for the A Journey of Riches series http://ajourneyofriches.com/ and his publishing house, Motion Media International, has published 28 non-fiction titles to date.

John also co-wrote and produced the movie documentary Adversity starring Jack Canfield, Rev. Micheal Bernard Beckwith, Dr. John Demartini and many more, coming soon in 2022. Moreover, you can bet there will be a best-selling book to follow!

"A spiritual awakening is not usually pleasant.

Often it feels like confusion, frustration, anger, sadness, grief, or being 'out of place'.

A spiritual awakening can be uncomfortable & challenging because it's an intense time of personal growth.

But despite how difficult it may feel, you're not going crazy: you're evolving."

~ Unknown

AFTERWORD

I hope you enjoyed the collection of heartfelt stories, wisdom and vulnerability shared. Storytelling is the oldest form of communication, and I hope you feel inspired to take a step toward living a fulfilling life. Feel free to contact any of the authors in this book, or the other books in this series.

The proceeds of this book will feed many of the rural Balinese families struggling through the current pandemic.

Other books in the series are…

The Power of Inspiration: A Journey of Riches, Book Twenty Seven
http://mybook.to/ThePowerofInspiration

Messages from The Heart: A Journey of Riches, Book Twenty Six
http://mybook.to/MessagesOfHeart

Abundant living: A Journey of Riches, Book Twenty Five
https://www.amazon.com/dp/B0963N6B2C

The Way of the Leader: A Journey of Riches, Book Twenty Four
https://www.amazon.com/dp/1925919285

The Attitude of Gratitude: *A Journey of Riches,* Book Twenty Three
https://www.amazon.com/dp/1925919269

Facing your Fears: *A Journey of Riches,* Book Twenty Two
https://www.amazon.com/dp/1925919218

Returning to Love: *A Journey of Riches,* Book Twenty One
https://www.amazon.com/dp/B08C54M2RB

Develop Inner Strength: *A Journey of Riches,* Book Twenty
https://www.amazon.com/dp/1925919153

Building your Dreams: A Journey of Riches, Book Nineteen
https://www.amazon.com/dp/B081KZCN5R

Liberate your Struggles: A Journey of Riches, Book Eighteen
https://www.amazon.com/dp/1925919099

In Search of Happiness: A Journey of Riches, Book Seventeen
https://www.amazon.com/dp/B07R8HMP3K

Tapping into Courage: A Journey of Riches, Book Sixteen
https://www.amazon.com/dp/B07NDCY1KY

The Power Healing: A Journey of Riches, Book Fifteen
https://www.amazon.com/dp/B07LGRJQ2S

The Way of the Entrepreneur: A Journey Of Riches, Book Fourteen
https://www.amazon.com/dp/B07KNHYR8V

Discovering Love and Gratitude: A Journey Of Riches, Book Thirteen
https://www.amazon.com/dp/B07H23Q6D1

Transformational Change: A Journey Of Riches, Book Twelve
https://www.amazon.com/dp/B07FYHMQRS

Finding Inspiration: A Journey Of Riches, Book Eleven
https://www.amazon.com/dp/B07F1LS1ZW

Building your Life from Rock Bottom: A Journey Of Riches,
Book Ten
https://www.amazon.com/dp/B07CZK155Z

Transformation Calling: A Journey Of Riches, Book Nine
https://www.amazon.com/dp/B07BWQY9FB

Letting Go and Embracing the New: A Journey Of Riches, Book
Eight
https://www.amazon.com/dp/B079ZKT2C2

Making Empowering Choices: A Journey Of Riches, Book Seven
https://www.amazon.com/Making-Empowering-Choices-Journey-
Riches-ebook/dp/B078JXMK5V

The Benefit of Challenge: A Journey Of Riches, Book Six
https://www.amazon.com/dp/B0778S2VBD

Personal Changes: A Journey Of Riches, Book Five
https://www.amazon.com/dp/B075WCQM4N

Dealing with Changes in Life: A Journey Of Riches, Book Four
https://www.amazon.com/dp/B0716RDKK7

Making Changes: A Journey Of Riches, Book Three
https://www.amazon.com/dp/B01MYWNI5A

The Gift In Challenge: A Journey Of Riches, Book Two
https://www.amazon.com/dp/B01GBEML4G

From Darkness into the Light: A Journey Of Riches, Book One
https://www.amazon.com/dp/B018QMPHJW

Afterword

Thank you to all the authors who have shared aspects of their lives, hoping to inspire others to live a bigger version of themselves. I heard a great saying from Jim Rohan, "You can't complain and feel grateful at the same time." At any given moment, we have a choice to either feel like a victim of life, or be connected and grateful for it. I hope this book helps you to feel grateful and inspires you to go after your dreams. For more information about contributing to the series, visit http://ajourneyofriches.com/. Furthermore, if you enjoyed reading this book, we would appreciate your review on Amazon to help get our message out to more readers.